Chords of Hope

Overcoming Common Musician Problems and Resting in God's Character through Hymns

Julie Crowe

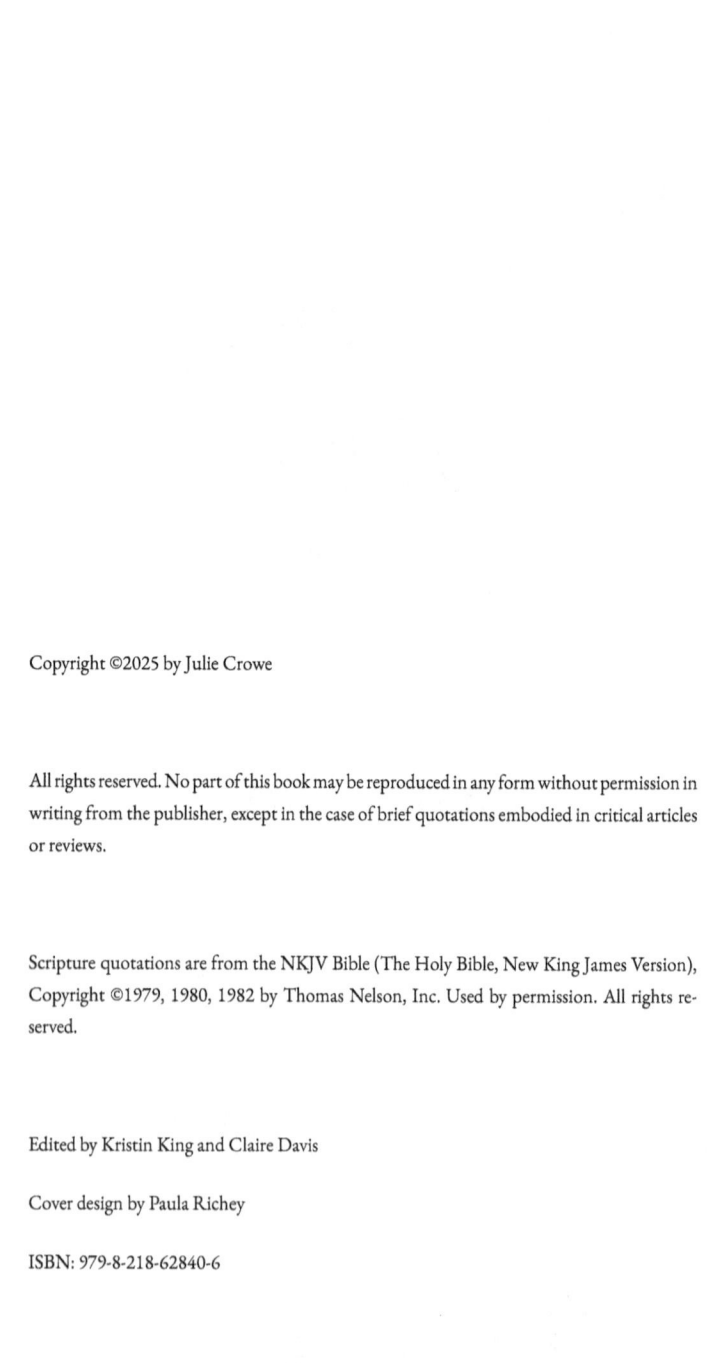

Edited by Kristin King and Claire Davis

Cover design by Paula Richey

ISBN: 979-8-218-62840-6

Contents

Dedication

For all who have a heart like Nancy:
Thank you. Keep working for the Lord. Your influences are powerful
in the building of God's Kingdom.

Foreword

Throughout the history of the Church, diverse subjects have been debated and contemplated. From the thorough discussions of the Nicene Creed and ecumenical councils to Thomas Aquinas and his great Summa Theologica, the Church has seen her fair share of intellectual rigor. Thankfully, this rigor and devotion seen in the ancient Church was not limited to their councils or synods; rather it stretched to their considerations on worship and praise. The basis for all these diverse considerations and debates were, of course, to be settled through Scripture.

As Augustine states, "For I confess to your Charity that I have learned to yield this respect and honour only to the canonical books of Scripture: of these alone do I most firmly believe that the authors were completely free from error" (Augustine's letter to Jerome 82.3). It is no surprise then that the early Church sought to establish the matter of worship and praise through the lens of the two Testaments of Scripture. Even earlier in Church history, Clement of Alexandria adds in the late second century, "For the apostle adds again, 'Teaching and admonishing one another in all wisdom, in psalms, and hymns, and spiritual songs, singing with grace in your heart to God.' And again, 'Whatsoever ye do in word or deed, do all in the name of the Lord Jesus, giving thanks to God and His Father.' This is our thankful revelry. And even if you wish to sing and play to the harp or lyre, there is no blame" (Ante-Nicene Fathers, vol. 1, p. 249).

The usage of music and instruments was often integral to the worship of the saints, even of those before the coming of Christ. Think of the musician David, as he leads a kingdom as the warrior-poet. His view, as well as many throughout the Church in history, has consistently shown the importance of worship and praises rightly directed. This thought is exactly the thought process behind the writing of this book. It serves as an introduction not only to the pitfalls and successes of musical worship, but also follows the consistent and solid practice of the Church.

This book serves as a guidepost to the wanderer, lost in the inconsistency of modern musical practice. While professing worship for God, often the modern thought finds worship of self to be always in the fine print of our musical scores. This idea, among many others, is addressed thoroughly in this book. The ideas found in this book, such as the dangers of pride, perfectionism, and feelings of inadequacy touch the heart of the Gospel itself.

As Paul states in what is often called his magnum opus of Romans, "And to the one who does not work but believes in him who justifies the ungodly, his faith is counted as righteousness" (Romans 4:5). It is by the grace of God alone that man is saved, and no amount of worship and practice can redeem a fallen soul. However, to the one who has ceased working for salvation and has trusted Christ's work, worship becomes a pleasure and not a task. To the one who rests and trusts in Him, they will find peace with God.

True worship, then, must be directed through a pure heart, without which no one will see God. Only when we work because of our salvation, and not for our salvation, will we ever find true and lasting peace in the art of music performance. I found this book to stand squarely in the stream of Christian thought and devotion. I pray that it will encourage your understanding of worship and musicianship as well.

Adam Boyce
Master of Divinity, 2023
Anderson University, South Carolina

"God is not a man, that He should lie, nor a son of man, that He should repent. Has He said, and will He not do? Or has He spoken, and will He not make it good?"

–Numbers 23:19

"To love at all is to be vulnerable. Love anything and your heart will certainly be wrung and possibly broken. If you want to make sure of keeping it intact, you must give your heart to no one, not even an animal. Wrap it carefully round with hobbies and little luxuries: avoid all entanglements; lock it up safe in the casket or coffin of your selfishness. But in that casket — safe, dark, motionless, airless — it will change. It will not be broken; it will become unbreakable, impenetrable."

-C. S. Lewis

Introduction

For as long as I can remember, I have always felt hymns were powerful, reassuring, and beautiful. They always reminded me of my grandparents' generation — how they seemingly breathed the breath of God. I always wondered what makes both hymns and older generations so different. To have that kind of relationship with God is incredible — it's something Christians today seem to lack. While we can't live the same lives as they did and grow up in the same world our grandparents knew, I do believe we can have more of "the breath of God" in and on us.

So much of God's character can be found in hymns. In my personal walk, I've found hymns are more about knowing God over anything else and how He can transform us and our unprocessed hurts. Hymns come from a place of deep emotion, including incredible love and deliverance. With hymns being built on a Biblical foundation, we are continuously pointed to the Creator of music.

It wasn't until I started deeply studying the hymns that I began to see God's character, which led to my perception of Him being transformed from an angry, distant God (although I knew deep down it wasn't true) to a loving and personal God. From there, I started experiencing more chains being broken and freedoms than I had before. From living as if I was already rejected and other spirit-crushing ways of looking at life, the Lord freed me when I called upon His Name -- I felt truly free for the first time in so long! I believe He is willing and able to do this for you, too!

When I felt the Lord leading me to study music in college, I faced so many difficult hurdles emotionally, technically, and socially. I was the ideal student growing up, but that quickly changed as I fought grief, the feeling of deep inadequacy, perfectionism, and unresolved trauma I didn't know I was carrying. I really didn't like most of the musical training at the time because I felt like all of it was just rigorous rules with little room for enjoyment. Eventually, I lost my drive for music.

While I couldn't personally relate to classical music or consider myself a classical violinist, I found my strength and a place to rest in Christian hymns. Eventually, I forged my own way in music despite feeling as if I could not succeed as a classically trained musician. I learned so much from those beautiful, ancient words of wisdom in hymns and stumbled upon my passion: helping others find and see the Lord as loving, good, and tender toward us. It is a winding, difficult road that I'm still walking as I cultivate my calling.

From one broken Christian musician to another, I sincerely hope this Gospel tract book, as I lovingly call it, inspires you to pick up your instrument again if you've set it aside for some reason. Use it to build His Kingdom musically and grow in deeper understanding of Him. I hope this book will allow you to see Him as loving and tender as He uses hymns to renovate your heart and mind. It is my utmost desire and prayer that the Lord uses my hardships to encourage and guide you on your own musical journey and walk with Him. Along the way you'll begin to see a sneak peek of how God perhaps intends to use music for us and others. May this book encourage you as you endeavor to seek Him with your whole heart and your music.

How to Use This Book

This book is not just another book to be read once and enjoyed (although I hope you do both). It is a book that needs your participation to truly get the most from it. At the end of each chapter, I've included Questions to Ponder. It may be helpful to write and reflect in a journal or notebook as you read.

At the conclusion of each chapter is a hymn with lyrics for you to read. After you've read through it, I have some suggestions on how you can incorporate each hymn into your own personal music study time and practice.

Please let me know how this book helps you cultivate your God-given gift of music.

CHAPTER ONE

Precious and Bitter Memories

"For by grace you have been saved through faith, and that not of yourselves; it is the gift of God, not of works, lest anyone should boast. For we are His workmanship, created in Christ Jesus for good works, which God prepared beforehand that we should walk in them."

-Ephesians 2:8-10

"It's time to get ready for bed," Granny said in her Southern drawl as she turned off the television. The clock read 11:00PM. I really didn't want to go to bed. At night, I always felt like I was staring into the face of God with my sinfulness ever before me. I had accepted Christ at a young age and was actively living for Him, but I always struggled with feeling like He was angry with me and didn't want much to do with me. That feeling consumed me at bedtime when I couldn't ignore it.

"Okay," I responded and reluctantly went to get myself ready for bed. After changing clothes and brushing my teeth, I climbed in under the cool, blue-trimmed patchwork blanket that laid across "my bed" in my grandparents' guest bedroom. I felt anxiety crowding in as I stared at the ceiling. I glanced at the clock again. 11:30 PM.

A few moments passed before I heard someone talking. I strained to listen, both hoping and dreading to hear the voice again. Then I recognized Granny's voice. I listened as she spoke the names of my parents, brother, and myself, aunt, uncle, and cousins into the night. Granny was praying for all of us!

I pulled the covers over my head, full of awe and thankfulness, while trying to hide from God, although I knew that wasn't a possibility. A few minutes later I heard Granny walk from the hallway bathroom to her room. I could hear her bed creak and sheets ruffle before quiet followed with Papa's snoring and heavy breathing. I lay in silence, trying to settle my racing thoughts. When I got comfortable and quieted my loud thoughts, I fell into blissful sleep, unsure how to process what I had just overheard.

There were several truths I believed in my heart (growing up and as an adult) to be absolutes:

- God is real
- Jesus is real and died for my sins and rose again
- Hell and Heaven are real places

- How God views me is not the same as my negative thoughts

- My grandparents and their generation knew God in an incredibly intimate way that many of us today do not

- Hymns are special and beautifully mysterious

- Finally, the love of my closest family toward me – regardless of one's choices or life's seasons – is unwavering

Despite these good things I knew to be true, I somehow still felt God was also mad and distant from me.

Someone I was close to hurt me deeply. Prior to this, I was completely blind to what the future would bring. We spent so much time together. This man cultivated in me a love for insects, the stars, and learning about the world around me. He played guitar and sang "You Are My Sunshine" and had a laugh as big as his stomach. We would race up our driveway and take rides in his old truck to get the daily newspaper, and he would always buy me a Dr. Pepper and let me pick out a candy bar. I wanted to be like him, even down to being left-handed; I was very dismayed and frustrated when I started elementary school and realized my left hand was uncomfortable to write with. He even led me to Christ one, warm, summer evening. I felt the lightest I had ever felt afterward, and pondered how God had done this work in my heart.

A year or two later, this same man began to disappear. It was little by little here and there until the person I had known before was totally gone. The precious time we spent together was relegated to memories. Out of fear of losing control, his life became about upholding appearances and not allowing imperfections and brokenness to shine through. His laughter was replaced with self-cursing, music was no longer played on his guitar, the stars ceased to shine, and the driveway races all but stopped. The person I loved so much and was closest to disappeared into his own world of pain and unresolved trauma. As a child, it broke my heart that my person disappeared.

Looking back on this today, it breaks my heart that he hurt so deeply and could not find a way to help himself get through the pain. He really did not know how to get help, and he believed that God could not help him.

Today, he has returned to his faith in Christ, but he has days that he believes that God has given up on him. When he came fully back to himself and all of us, I emotionally collapsed and was left to work out what I had learned to be "true."

Along the way, I absorbed several false beliefs. I thought I had to be "good" and perfect, in my grades and music; I quaked in fear because God is distant and allows anything to happen to people; I was a people-pleaser; I believed that God is angry with me and I will always be in trouble, and perhaps the most painful lie of all: I am completely, deeply, and personally rejected. Whether the man who hurt me lived by these fake truths or not, I learned these beliefs in that environment which affected my personal thinking and my musical journey. I understood then that he was unable to process things that hurt him deeply; but in those years, I picked up some of those false beliefs as if they were my own to carry. I didn't recognize until years later that I was dealing with a form of childhood trauma.

In a childhood trauma and religiosity study conducted in 2020, researchers found that:

"...several studies have shown that a secure adult attachment was associated with a more positive image of God and a feeling towards God [26,33]. In contrast, avoidant attachment was related to the lack of a secure, positive relationship to God, a desire to keep God at a distance [34] and to the image of God as controlling or unavailable [33]. Similarly, anxious attachment was associated with an experience of abandonment or punishment by God as a projection of a personal attachment style [34] and with anxious attachment to God [30]. Thus, adult attachment may be likely relevant in forming one's God image."[1]

Comparatively, in Alisa Childers' and Tim Barnett's book, The Deconstruction of Christianity, we find a lot that is said about our culture on feelings and thoughts:

"We are all prone to imagine a God that is more like our culture or ourselves, than Who God truly is. If we're not careful, this can distort our view of Him."[2]

---

1. Kosarkova, Alice, Klara Malinakova, Jitse P. Van Dijk, and Peter Tavel. "Childhood Trauma and Experience in Close Relationships Are Associated with the God Image: Does Religiosity Make a Difference?" International Journal of Environmental Research and Public Health 17, no. 23 (November 28, 2020). https://doi.org/10.3390/ijerph17238841. Accessed on July 7, 2023.

2. Alisa Childers and Tim Barnett, The Deconstruction of Christianity: What It Is, Why It's Destructive, and How to Respond. Audiobook. (Tyndale Elevate, 2024). Chapter 3: Rerun. Accessed on February 19, 2024.

This quote is speaking on modern deconstruction where people are tearing down their childhood faith and walking away, but I also believe it applies to the hurt and pain-filled eyes of those who struggle to see God as good. I have talked to many people who went through similar things I experienced, and I can't help but wonder if pain and hurt walk together with deconstruction. I had to personally come face to face with my pain and unravel its roots deeply entangled in my heart and mind.

Still, I held tightly to my faith, knowing in my heart that the Lord is real and believing He is loving, despite my feelings or what I perceived growing up. This is not to say, "Look at me; I've got it all figured out now." Because I don't. It comes from a place of deep-set stubbornness and believing all I was raised to suppose is right and true. I've come to the other side of the pain and I'm here to say that you don't have to see God with the same characteristics of the person who hurt you deeply. I've come to realize that the only way those safely guarded places could begin to be reached and touched was through my grandparents who were saved by grace through Jesus, through others like them, and through Scripture-based hymns.

God used music to touch my heart and help reach those dark places I didn't want anyone else to access. As I changed, I found a whole new level of grace. I've come to realize so many others are walking around hurting beyond what we can see or fathom.

From a 2019 study on Music Psychology, Music Therapy, and Worship Music:

> "University of the Highlands and Islands professor Michael Lowis conducted a study in which men and women in the church (namely ordained ministers and qualified members of the congregation) were asked

to rate how important hymns were to religious ser-
vices and...After the study was complete, Lowis found
that...leaders found worship music helpful for speaking aspects of God's healing and reminding people
that they are children of a faithful God who is capable
of bringing healing regardless of their situation."[3]

It is my opinion that people living today in First World Countries
have forgotten God cannot sin. We have lowered our expectations of
God to be the same as that of the sins of men and instead raised up
the goodness of men to be faultless and ultimately glorified pain as
an excuse and a badge of honor. This results in making God sinful
and man is perfect and is acceptable for man to wallow in the excuses of pain indefinitely. This is not what many would call "fair."
However, brokenness can be redeemed into beauty when we separate
the "sinfulness" man has incorrectly assigned to God and make God
inherently good again instead of evil, and men inherently evil from
birth, instead of inherently good. Our emotions and feelings are not
dictators. They are indicators, but are misleading and can be liars.

None of us are lost causes, but we must acknowledge that only God
can work repentance in our hearts that brings real and lasting transfor-
mation, including that of assigning God as sinful and evil because of
our pain we experience in life. There are no excuses. However, I believe
one of the avenues He uses to continue to reach out to all mankind –
including those who call Him names that He is not – is through music.
A relationship with God through Jesus is the start of your way out of

3. Whittemore, Jessica. "A Study of Music: Music Psychology, Music Therapy,
and Worship Music." Senior Thesis, Liberty University, 2019. Accessed on
July 7, 2023.

a life of sin, hurt, and pain. Music and connection with Himself are incredible gifts He gives.

Questions to Ponder:

• What precious memories do you have about loved ones who loved the Lord? What set them apart? Why were you close to them?

• What bitter memories do you have that may have driven you away from the Lord? Why did these things push you away? Is there a way you can find your way back to the Lord again?

• Where are you currently in your faith walk with God?

Come, Ye Sinners, Poor and Needy
(J Hart, 1759)

1. Come, ye sinners, poor and needy,
weak and wounded, sick and sore;
Jesus ready stands to save you,
full of pity, love and pow'r.

2. Come, ye thirsty, come, and welcome,
God's free bounty glorify;
true belief and true repentance,
ev'ry grace that brings you nigh.

3. Let not conscience make you linger,
nor of fitness fondly dream;
all the fitness He requireth
is to feel your need of Him.

4. Come, ye weary, heavy laden,
lost and ruined by the fall;
if you tarry till you're better,
you will never come at all.

5. Lo! th'incarnate God, ascended,
pleads the merit of His blood;
venture on Him, venture wholly;
let no other trust intrude.

"Come, Ye Sinners, Poor and Needy," Hymnary.org, n.d., https://hymnary.org/text/come_ye_sinners_poor_and_needy_weak_and. Accessed on July 1, 2023.

Hymn Study

1. Look up the backstory to this hymn. What strikes you most?

2. Now, look up the music to this hymn and play through it. It is necessary to understand lyrics and hear the music. Don't just play through it with no thought. Really think about what is being conveyed in this hymn.

3. Look up arrangements of this hymn by various artists on YouTube. Which arrangements do you gravitate to?

4. What do you feel like you gained from this hymn?

5. What do you perceive from this hymn about the Lord's character?

Thoughts/Notes/Prayers:

CHAPTER TWO

The Truth About Pride

"Two are better than one, because they have a good reward for their labor. For if they fall, one will lift up his companion. But woe to him who is alone when he falls, for he has no one to help him up. Again, if two lie down together, they will keep warm; but how can one be warm alone?"

-Ecclesiastes 4:9-11

Balancing a healthy amount of self-confidence in your music is hard to navigate. Too much, and you will encounter pride, maybe even hubris. Too little, and your playing suffers from timidity. Even overt humility can be a form of pride. This deadly sin distracts us from what is important and sets us up as our own god.

I used to think I wasn't prideful. You might say I prided myself on my humility. I thought I had to forge my own way, leaving God out of the equation and anticipating it all would go the way I wanted. I thought He was not as concerned about what happened in my day-to-day life, that He was only a passive participant in my life, or He would somehow ruin what I wanted. So, I never surrendered much to Him. It hurt to let Him in to my vulnerable and broken places, so I didn't. I felt like God couldn't be trusted with things that were important to me. I was afraid He would shut down things out of His control, not love and care.

After listening to Jennie Allen's audiobook, *Get Out of Your Head: Stopping the Spiral of Toxic Thoughts*[1] , the Holy Spirit revealed to me how prideful I can be. Pride has many forms, and some of them are more obvious than others, such as the musician who has clearly worked hard, no doubt, for their chair position but makes you uncomfortable to be around because of their superior demeanor. But there's also a pride of thinking, "I can personally handle anything that comes my way." I can find myself wanting to control, manipulate, please, and make things happen on my own musically or personally.

I can easily allow my people-pleasing and anxiety to come out and take over. My desires become idols that derail me from my relationship with God and others. I feel the need to pick up things and bear them alone, not letting anyone get through the high walls I've constructed ever so carefully. I can't stand for someone to see me at my most vulnerable state. This is the way I lived my life for so long and still struggle to remember that "God directs his steps..." (Proverbs 16:9).

---

1. Allen, Jennie. *Get Out of Your Head: Stopping the Spiral of Toxic Thoughts.* WaterBrook, 2020. Accessed on June 23, 2022.

My false sense of control over every little thing in my life must be given over daily to the Lord.

Can you relate? Have you ever dealt with a problem of pride masquerading as false humility? You think, "I have to carry it all, and I have to do it perfectly."

This can be the case in music, too. You are only capable of so much, and what you have succeeded and mastered is not "yours." You don't carve out your own path. I've found that if it's not what we are supposed to be doing, that door shuts on our pursuits. But anything that is God-ordained, He always makes a way.

Ephesians 2:2 talks about Satan having the power of the air. I interpret that to be anything that is heard via social media, television, spoken words, and anything else that travels through the air, including music. We can take the good things God has made and make them bad. That's why it is so important to fill our minds with God's Word.

Choosing to allow God to be God and the Author and Giver of everything we have is freeing. It has allowed me to live a more peaceful and God-focused life. It's like Jennie Allen states in her book, Get Out of Your Head (and in Scripture) that we must take every thought captive to Christ (2 Corinthians 10:5) and that we have the power to make our thoughts be obedient to Christ.[2]

God tells us to "pray without ceasing" in 1 Thessalonians 5:7. I think hymns are a good second to this, because hymns are filled with theology and built on Biblical truths. Hymns also show us how we can be humble. Perhaps it is knowing how down-to-earth those past generations were, but the songwriters knew how to reverence the Lord and live humbly. They realized they have no control over anything that

---

2. Allen, Jennie. Get Out of Your Head: Stopping the Spiral of Toxic Thoughts. WaterBrook, 2020.

happens. They didn't even have all that we do today with modern medicine. They depended solely on the Lord for all they needed. While modern medicine can only do so much, God is our ultimate Healer.

Have you ever spoken with an elder loved one who knows the Lord? They are often saturated with humility. I think the best way we can begin to attain that same humility is to live our lives in total surrender, knowing that He is a God of love. We can also start reading the hymns and playing them. They are so powerful the words seem to breathe life back into brittle, pride-ridden hearts.

God is not like us. He's not sinful and ugly toward us. He didn't set the world in motion just to watch it unfold for His entertainment. He truly loves and cares for His creation. He is not like that person that hurt you; in fact, He is not that person. He cannot hurt us because it is against His literal Being. I stopped seeing The Lord as a passive, impersonal deity when I started reading the hymns and filling my mind with their declarations of faith. I knew in my heart that my grandparents' and parents' Christian beliefs were the Absolute Truth, but my eyesight had previously been too contaminated with the ugliness that flows from others and my own toxic sludge that would seep out from time to time.

People fail us. We fail others, and honestly, we fail ourselves. So how can you be both confident and truly humble? How do you pluck pride from your life?

Know your strengths and celebrate them. Know your weaknesses and work on those by giving yourself tons of grace. Cheer on those who are musically more advanced than you are, and encourage those who aren't as good or as far enough along as you were yesterday; but most importantly, remember it's not all about you. Be still and remember that God is God (Psalm 46:10) and come to Him multiple times a day in prayer (1 Thessalonians 5:17) or singing.

We may have an innate musical ability that we work hard to develop, but we didn't give it to ourselves. The gift of music is always meant to point back to the Giver. And our weaknesses require us to remember we can't do it all on our own. We must rely on the Lord to carry it out when we have nothing more in us. We see that with Paul:

> "And lest I should be exalted above measure by the abundance of the revelations, a thorn in the flesh was given to me, a messenger of Satan to buffet me, lest I be exalted above measure. Concerning this thing I pleaded with the Lord three times that it might depart from me. And He said to me, 'My grace is sufficient for you, for My strength is made perfect in weakness.' Therefore most gladly will I rather boast in my infirmities, that the power of Christ may rest upon me. Therefore I take pleasure in infirmities, in reproaches, in needs, in persecutions, in distresses, for Christ's sake. For when I am weak, then I am strong."
>
> -2 Corinthians 12:7-10

When you allow the vulnerability in yourself to meet with your confidence in the Lord, He will help you cope as you surrender your whole heart to Him. You begin settling into who you truly are. Your strengths and weaknesses make up who you are musically, too. Seasons of life come and go, along with practicing schedules and you get comfortable in your own treble, bass, or alto clef pitched voice on the path that God has set before you, while constantly allowing Him to tune it to a pitch that most resembles His heart.

Questions to Ponder:

• Where have you been prideful spiritually and musically?

• How can you begin to let go of what you think you can control and leave it in God's hands instead?

• What does pride look like?

• What does humility look like?

Turn Your Eyes Upon Jesus
(Helen Howarth Lemmel, 1922)

1. O soul, are you weary and troubled?
No light in the darkness you see?
There's light for a look at the Savior,
And life more abundant and free!

Refrain:
Turn your eyes upon Jesus,
Look full in His wonderful face,
And the things of earth will grow strangely dim,
In the light of His glory and grace.

2. Thro' death into life everlasting,
He passed, and we follow Him there;
O'er us sin no more hath dominion--
For more than conqu'rors we are!

3. His Word shall not fail you--He promised;
Believe Him, and all will be well:
Then go to a world that is dying,
His perfect salvation to tell!

Hymnary.org. "Turn Your Eyes upon Jesus," n.d. https://hymnary.org/text/o_soul_are_you_weary_and_troubled. Accessed on July 1, 2023.

Hymn Study

1. Look up the backstory to this hymn. What strikes you most?

2. Now, look up the music to this hymn and play through it. It is necessary to understand lyrics and hear the music. Don't just play through it with no thought. Really think about what is being conveyed in this hymn.

3. Look up arrangements of this hymn by various artists on YouTube. Which arrangements do you gravitate to?

4. What do you feel like you gained from this hymn?

5. What do you perceive from this hymn about the Lord's character?

Thoughts/Notes/Prayers:

CHAPTER THREE

Perfectionism and Constructive Criticism

"Therefore, whether you eat or drink, or whatever you do, do all to the glory of God."

-1 Corinthians 10:31

Perfectionism is one of the biggest, oxymoronic issues of our time, especially when it comes to our music practice. Some qualities are expected and needed (such as good intonation or good playing and holding technique), but we have become so focused on these qualities that we have inadvertently lost sight of the overall beauty of (imperfect) music. The human body and ability levels are all diverse. An 81-year-old will not be able to hold the violin the way a 20-year-old can. In an age where appearance is all too important, it is difficult to refrain from judging others. Every single person out there is doing their best, but what happens when it's not good enough?

Perfectionism has become a form of control. In Matthew 5:48, Jesus states, "Therefore, you shall be perfect, just as your Father in heaven is perfect." At first glance, it appears that we must operate as perfect in our sin-laden bodies. But a closer look at Ellicott's Commentary gives us new insight to perfection:

> "...The idea of perfection implied in the word is that of the attainment of the end or ideal completeness of our being. In us that attainment implies growth, and the word is used (e.g., in 1 Corinthians 2:6; Hebrews 5:14) of men of full age as contrasted with infants. In God the perfection is not something attained, but exists eternally, but we draw near to it and become partakers of the divine nature when we love as He loves..." [1]

This is talking about spiritual maturity, but it can also be applied to music. This growth is evident in older generations and in the hymns those people created. It is especially evident over the course of our lives and how life experiences and trials are used to shape us. We never become perfect here on earth — not by conduct, by the things we do, or by how many hours of practice we put in. We are broken people living in a broken and messy world. Obtaining perfection of any kind

---

1. Matthew 5:48 Commentaries: "Therefore You Are to Be Perfect, as Your Heavenly Father Is Perfect.," n.d. https://biblehub.com/commentaries/matthew/5-48.htm.

is fruitless and time-wasting. We will only be perfect in Heaven, but anything here does need to be given our best, in the season we are in. Easier said than done, I know.

People with full-time jobs will not have as much time to devote to practicing as full-time students. A full-time student will have to divide their time between classes, practicing, mental health, and social life. Difficult seasons of life will further complicate finding that balance. In every season, we can still give our best effort to the music practice we're able to get and leave the rest at Jesus' feet.

We learn from the hard days and seasons and allow these times to grow and develop us. We worship God through it all because, as Lysa TerKeurst says, "worship changes us."[2] Music is supposed to reflect real life, from real composers. Heartbreaks, true love realized and reciprocated, and total dejection can be represented in the staves. When you replace authenticity with perfectionism, you get falsehood and emptiness.

As a junior in college, I went through a difficult time emotionally and personally; my people-pleasing and emotional abandonment tendencies convinced me I needed the awe and approval of my professors. To draw out my best, I practiced to the point of exhaustion. I came to a point where I gave everything I had to developing my musical efforts, and I soon found myself maxed out. I had nothing more to give. The more I aimed to please my professors, the bigger deficit I created in myself.

---

2. TerKeurst, Lysa. "When I'm Desperate for God to Give Me All of the Details..." Https://Www.Facebook.Com/OfficialLysa/Photos/a.42752036 7693/10156895055707694/?Type=3, June 5, 2021. Accessed April 18, 2022. https://www.facebook.com/OfficialLysa/photos/a.427520367693/ 10156895055707694/?type=3

During my senior year, I came to a point where I had to let go of the "control" in my playing and the responses of others. I had to change my thinking before I completely broke. In Performance Seminar class, I learned to listen to the feedback given, process it carefully, and let the constructive criticism go before I took it as a personal deficit. I knew I had done my best, practiced, and performed for God's glory. Each performance belonged to God, the good and the bad, the slip-ups, the rhythms I liked to make up that weren't there, and the bad intonation of a nervous shift. This release of control helped me get through sc hool.

Hymns quickly became my worship and comfort because they never demanded perfection. Their only demands were for me to be still before God and play as skillfully as I could. The hymns felt safe, and as a result, I felt safe. That's why I love church music so much and even teach hymns in private lessons.

Doing your best is important, but you are allowed to make mistakes because you are human. Just give yourself grace! God uses what little we have of ourselves to speak to others in a personal way through our abilities and even our mistakes. You never know how the Holy Spirit is working in someone's life because of your music!

Sometimes it can be difficult to receive criticism about music be-cause it can be a deeply personal line of connection to God. Inviting others to hear your most heartfelt playing is scary. It's a place where improvement, talking with God, and being vulnerable often meet. It's your choice in how you will handle your sensitivities and know where your boundaries are. Any time you choose the Lord as a safe harbor and look at things through His perspective, it's always a good place to abide. It's important to develop good technical, tonal, and rhythmic foundations. Develop your signature musical style, but beyond that:

• Play with excellence

- Play from the heart
- Play for the Lord
- Minister and be ministered to

I have to think that this could be the heart of God when He created music.

Questions to Ponder:

- Do you think you're a perfectionist? Why or why not?
- How can you begin to abstain from maintaining or seeking perfectionism in the future?
- What keeps you grounded?
- What is your next step, musically and personally?

Never Alone
(Anonymous)

1 I've seen the lightning flashing
And heard the thunder roll,
I've felt sin's breakers dashing,
which tried to conquer my soul;
I've heard the voice of my Savior,
He bid me still fight on:
He promised never to leave me,
Never to leave me alone.

Refrain:
No, never alone,
No, never alone;
He promised never to leave me,
Never to leave me alone.

2 The world's fierce winds are blowing–
Temptation's sharp and keen;
I have a peace in knowing
My Savior stands between;
He stands to shield me from danger
When all my friends are gone:
He promised never to leave me,
Never to leave me alone. [Refrain]

(Cont.)

3 When in affliction's valley
I tread the road of care,
My Savior helps me carry
My cross so heavy to bear;
Though all around me is darkness
And earthly joys are flown,
My Savior whispers His promise:
Never to leave me alone. [Refrain]

4 He died on Calv'ry's mountain,
For me they pierced His side,
For me He opened that fountain,
The crimson, cleansing tide;
For me He's waiting in glory
Upon His heavenly throne:
He promised never to leave me,
Never to leave me alone. [Refrain]

Hymnary.org. "Never Alone," n.d. https://hymnary.org/text/ive_seen_the_lightning_
flashing. Accessed on June 30, 2023.

Hymn Study

1. Look up the backstory to this hymn. What strikes you most?

2. Now, look up the music to this hymn and play through it. It is necessary to understand lyrics and hear the music. Don't just play through it with no thought. Really think about what is being conveyed in this hymn.

3. Look up arrangements of this hymn by various artists on YouTube. Which arrangements do you gravitate to?

4. What do you feel like you gained from this hymn?

5. What do you perceive from this hymn about the Lord's character?

Thoughts/Notes/Prayers:

CHAPTER FOUR

People–Pleasing... Is It Worth It?

"For do I now persuade men, or God? Or do I seek to please men? For if I still pleased men, I would not be a bondservant of Christ."

-Galatians 1:10

"Let not your heart be troubled; you believe in God, believe also in Me."

-John 14:1

People-pleasing has always been a snare for me that I've had to gradually let go as I've grown in my faith. I always aimed to make good grades in school, and being given "star"-like roles in music would earn me a hearty pat on the back from my dad, someone I always aimed to please. When I felt I had let my professors down or reached my personal limit of what I could provide musically, the ground beneath my feet trembled. I reasoned that if I could only do everything to a "T", it would remedy this. I was trying to please everyone I encountered, when in reality, I cannot be all for everyone. I'm not Jesus. I can't fill that hole or make anyone else's life complete. I didn't realize that for a long time I elevated people and demoted God.

People-pleasing is a hunger that will never quite be satisfied, and it will never complete you. It will leave you wanting more because you can never get enough of everyone's approval. It will drain away your joy and lead to burnout.

In the music world, it's all too easy to fall in the trap of people-pleasing behavior. How do you know when playing expressively is enough? How do you know what is right, interpretatively? Well, you don't. There is no one, definite interpretation of music. We can look at the Baroque era and know that they didn't use vibrato when they played and emulate that. Playing from different eras (even Contemporary), it ultimately comes down to how a person interprets the music they're playing. We all come from different walks, and we all have different ways of looking at the world. So, you have to use your best judgement based on what you know from that era of music history.

I recently saw a video on the Facebook page Cross Examined in which Melissa Dougherty was answering the question of "What's the oldest lie in the book?" Dougherty explains that people set themselves up on their own throne as the god of themselves and their world and that God can give us "godlike authority in order to do what He does." She goes on to explain that people elevating themselves and demoting God leads to the consequence of building the Kingdom of Man instead of the Kingdom of God.[1] This is a big problem today! We do it more than we realize or would like to acknowledge.

It's easy to measure God against people when we are hurt by them. You may have an amazing friend who eventually fails or hurts you in some way. If you've elevated that person by looking to find your fulfillment, acceptance, and relief in them, you'll be crushed when they fall short of perfection. This situation can cause you to somehow believe God will treat you the same way, and it causes you to mistrust God in the same way that you now mistrust that friend.

Numbers 23:19 says, "God is not a man, that He should lie, Nor a son of man, that He should repent. Has He said, and will He not do? Or has He spoken, and will He not make it good?"

What do we get from this? Simply that God is not a man and cannot sin. What He says, He will do! This verse has become one of my favorite Bible verses. When I coupled it with studying hymns, it truly changed my life!

Hymns are filled with Theology. Jingles from commercials can stick with you for years. There is a whole branch of music that helps others in the form of therapy. Hymns pierce the heart and can help change you from the inside out. There is such power in them through the intention and hearts of the person(s) who composed them. Many of the hymn writers put their faith and testimony to music. That's why grandparents and older generations of Christians are so important. They help us find and see God for who He was, is, and always will be.

---

1. Dougherty, Melissa. "What's the Oldest Lie in the Book? With Melissa Dougherty." CrossExamined.Org FB Group (Official), July 1, 2023. Accessed July 1, 2023. https://www.facebook.com/groups/1571557166387771/.

Back to the story I related in Chapter 1. I experienced some deep emotional hurts as a child from that person leaving my life. Addiction took over from his own unresolved hurts and pains. I knew he still loved me, and the person he'd become wasn't who he truly was. I knew the situation was complicated, even at a young age, but it still affected me. While I wish it didn't happen, God used it for my good. I'm here today telling you how I got through people-pleasing and seeing God as good again.

I worked through what I could on my own but could not break some of the deep-seated pains I learned from that person and others growing up. When that deep-set rejection felt like it was eating me from the inside out that I was being devoured alive I cried out to the Lord and He saved me from it. God did the real heart work in me.

In music, people-pleasing, perfectionism, and a sprinkle of fear fuel one another in a vicious cycle. I had to lessen the grip gradually and let go of my need to please others to be healthier mentally and musically one day at a time, one small thing at a time. I still want to be perfect and not show how I struggle with rhythms, or how I'm out of sync when I'm in an orchestra these days, and how I struggle to play a solo piece with a piano accompanying me. It's uncomfortable, but those broken things make me real and keep me relying on the One Who completes me in every part of my life.

While we should always strive to make ourselves better musicians and Christians, this process lasts a lifetime. We will never achieve perfection this side of heaven. People's opinions, even well meaning, educated ones, come and go; but God's love for us is everlasting.

It's because of Jesus that you are enough, right here, where you are. You can get caught up in the pats on the back from others, but they do not fill you. They're like potato chips, tasty, but otherwise empty and void of nutrition. Quiet your heart, fellow musician, and be still.

Allow God to meet you in the silence and on stage in front of your audience; at the wedding you're playing at or at home in the comfort of your practice room. Do your best for God and worship Him. It's all for His glory anyway.

Questions to Ponder:
- Are you a people-pleaser?
- If so, can you think of something that set that tendency to please others into motion?
- Has people-pleasing benefitted you in any way?
- Why does it seemingly hurt more when other Christians let us down?

Just a Closer Walk with Thee
(Anonymous)

1 I am weak but Thou art strong;

Jesus, keep me from all wrong;

I'll be satisfied as long

As I walk, let me walk close to Thee.

Refrain:

Just a closer walk with Thee,

Grant it, Jesus, is my plea,

Daily walking close to Thee,

Let it be, dear Lord, let it be.

2 Thro' this world of toil and snares,

If I falter, Lord, who cares?

Who with me my burden shares?

None but Thee, dear Lord, none but Thee. [Refrain]

3 When my feeble life is o'er,

Time for me will be no more;

Guide me gently, safely o'er

To Thy kingdom shore, to Thy shore. [Refrain]

Hymnary.org. "Just a Closer Walk With Thee," n.d. https://hymnary.org/text/i_am_weak_but_thou_art_strong. Accessed on July 1, 2023.

Hymn Study

1. Look up the backstory to this hymn. What strikes you most?

2. Now, look up the music to this hymn and play through it. It is necessary to understand lyrics and hear the music. Don't just play through it with no thought. Really think about what is being conveyed in this hymn.

3. Look up arrangements of this hymn by various artists on YouTube. Which arrangements do you gravitate to?

4. What do you feel like you gained from this hymn?

5. What do you perceive from this hymn about the Lord's character?

Thoughts/Notes/Prayers:

Chapter Five

The Art of Being Still

"Be still, and know that I am God; I will be exalted among the nations, I will be exalted in the earth!"

-Psalm 46:10

"The essence of sin is man substituting himself for God, while the essence of salvation is God substituting himself for man." [1]

-John Stott

1. "The Essence of Sin Is Man Substituting Himself for God, While the Essence of Salvation Is God Substituting Himself for Man." CrossExamined.Org FB Group (Official), June 28, 2022. Accessed June 30, 2023. https://www.facebook.com/photo/?fbid=3073311632934649&set=a.1376576842608145.

After leaving my children with my parents-in-law for a few hours to conduct violin lessons, I pulled up to my next student's house. I knew Nancy from church, but through our lessons, a friendship had blossomed. I got my violin, notebook, music duet book, and hymnal out of my car before walking to the front door. I waited at the glass door until I saw the front door open. I always glanced at Nancy's "From the Swing" painting someone painted for her that overlooked the swing in her sunroom.

The front door opened, and I stepped in to greet Nancy. "Hey, Julie. How are you?" her voice quivered but was filled with delight. She turned slowly to catch her balance on the doorway and held on to the furniture as she walked. After our usual exchanges, we settled in and caught up while we tuned our violins. Then we opened the lesson with a prayer and began to practice. We chatted a bit more about life before it was time for me to leave. This is how my lessons with Nancy often unfolded.

We always played hymns; we both desired to do so. It was at this point that I was beginning to step away from strictly classical music in my teaching to incorporating more hymns in the lessons, and Nancy certainly influenced my perception of the Lord and music. It was with her that I caught a glimpse of God working in the quiet of my heart, as if He were reaching out for me through her faith, words, and mannerisms. It would be a year or later before I called Nancy to talk more in depth about her walk with God.

"How were you taught about God when you were growing up?" I asked her over the phone one night.[2]

"Well," Nancy began, "Daddy always taught us that God is a loving God, and we should also respect Him." The words stuck with me as well as the differences of childrearing in Christian homes 70+ years ago versus today. Strict, but loving families helped carve the Christian grandparents we love and continue to ache for long after they're gone.

Why do we miss them so? Could it be that their character and love given so freely to us mirror a similar love God has for us? I tend to think that is a contributing factor. Do we teach our children enough that He is so loving, but also worthy of our respect? Maybe, maybe not. It's hard to say, as the times are as different as night is from day. Stopping for lessons and ending them with duets with Nancy always reminded me how we need to slow down to take things in.

I always find myself looking back on those times and thinking of the serenity of just slowing down and reflecting on the Lord with Nancy through music. It was just what my heart needed.

I was taught early on that rests in music are important. To me, they remind us to be still. No, I don't mean just with musical rests. How

---

2. Nancy, interview. September of 2020.

can we be still in music? Perhaps, we can take a moment to still our hearts before we engage in the music before us.

Hymns, or worship music in general, can connect us with the Lord perhaps touching the hearts and minds of people more intimately than most genres (because what other musical genre seeks the Lord?).[3]

So how can you attain this musical stillness? Play each note intentionally as if God was sitting with you; don't aim to please or make your playing perfect, but lay your heart open before God. Invite God into the practice room that hidden place you feel most comfortable, yet vulnerable. All artists lay their heart out on the line every time they play, sing, paint, or write. We are brave yet so sensitive. The Lord already sees and knows every strength and weakness about you, both musically and as a person. He loves every bit of you.

When you invite Him into that practice session even for just scales–it's about that relationship with Him: worshipping Him and playing for Him, instead of man. Your focus shifts from pleasing man (or even yourself) to prayerfully playing for Him. It melts a potential idol and frustration into nothing.

As you practice, ask God to join you. Say something to Him like, "I want You to listen to this and tell me what You think." It's about taking the focus off you and your music and making it about God. Practice as you normally would. That mental shift of playing outward to upward is both freeing and scary. Inviting anyone into our art is hard, but to invite the Creator of art and your heart? Worth it. He wants to be invited in. It's not about you. It's about how He can transform and use you, even in music.

---

3. Whittemore, Jessica. "A Study of Music: Music Psychology, Music Therapy, and Worship Music." Senior Thesis, Liberty University, 2019.

I've practiced this same process of inviting God into my music sessions. After I graduated college, I hated practicing. The voices of what I should have done better or differently would drown out my joy in music-making, and I would just practice a literal moment before giving up and putting my violin away because I still aimed to please others and myself. I lived this way for years. It wasn't until I invited God into my playing and asked Him to listen as I played the cello one night. It had been a hit-or-miss mess when I played in the past. Some of my muscle memory was "off." On this occasion, though, I asked God to come and sit with me and enjoy the sounds of my instrument as I played.

I took things slow. My bowing and fingering were deliberate. I played through a piece I had been practicing off and on for a few years. Nothing was rushed, because I was intentionally taking my time to be still. As a result, my practice session was the best I had ever played in around 8 years. Had I played like I normally did while allowing deeply critiquing voices ebbing in and out of my head because I set them up as a god, it would have torn me apart yet again, and I would have put away my cello quickly.

In Lysa TerKeurst's Trustworthy Bible study, she talks about how "God's word must lead my thoughts, not the other way around" and goes on to say that our motives must be what the Bible says, that we need to internalize and make it personal, "renovating" our temple for the Holy Spirit (p. 170, 173, 176).[4] Jennie Allen also talks in her book, Get Out of Your Head, about how we roughly have 30,000 thoughts

---

4. TerKeurst, Lysa. Trustworthy: Overcoming Our Greatest Struggles to Trust God. p. 170; 173; 176. LIfeway Press, 2019. Accessed on December 19, 2019.

a day, maybe more.[5] Allen said that it all boils down to capturing a thought, bringing it to Christ (2 Corinthians 10:5), and allowing Him to transform our minds (Romans 12:1-2).

These excellent points about how God should be the presiding voice in our heads can apply to how we treat our music as well. Holding on to the lie that we are undeserving or unloving can have some deep roots. It wasn't until recently that I found that we can seek freedom from these things when we stop to look at the small acts of love around us.

As my husband may do little things to show his love to me through small acts of service and kindness, I have realized in order to minimize these feelings being undeserving or unloving of God's love, we have to look at ourselves the way God sees us and look at the small little "petty" things that we prayed for and received from Him. This has been critical to begin to erase those feelings. If we are listening to the wrong voices, we are more apt to fail and ultimately live in some deep-set burnout and lies.

What if we did renovate our minds—how would that make a difference in our perception of music? How could you get to know Him better? Allow yourself to be still. Invite God in, even when it's scary or painful. Play for Him. Thank Him for the gift of music in your life.

Questions to Ponder:

• How can you "be still" before the Lord? What places do you need to practice this?

• How can you "be still" before the Lord, musically?

• How often will you practice this when you play?

• What do you expect to gain from this? What did you actually gain from this?

• How can you begin to accept God's love for you? What small steps can you commit to today?

Just As I Am
(Charlotte Elliott)

1 Just as I am, without one plea,
but that thy blood was shed for me,
and that thou bidd'st me come to thee,
O Lamb of God, I come, I come.

2 Just as I am, and waiting not
to rid my soul of one dark blot,
to thee, whose blood can cleanse each spot,
O Lamb of God, I come, I come.

3 Just as I am, though tossed about
with many a conflict, many a doubt,
fightings and fears within, without,
O Lamb of God, I come, I come.

4 Just as I am, thou wilt receive,
wilt welcome, pardon, cleanse, relieve;
because thy promise I believe,
O Lamb of God, I come, I come.

Hymnary.org. "Just as I Am, Without One Plea," n.d. https://hymnary.org/text/just_as_i_am_without_one_plea. Accessed on June 30, 2023.

Hymn Study

1. Look up the backstory to this hymn. What strikes you most?

2. Now, look up the music to this hymn and play through it. It is necessary to understand lyrics and hear the music. Don't just play through it with no thought. Really think about what is being conveyed in this hymn.

3. Look up arrangements of this hymn by various artists on YouTube. Which arrangements do you gravitate to?

4. What do you feel like you gained from this hymn?

5. What do you perceive from this hymn about the Lord's character?

Thoughts/Notes/Prayers:

CHAPTER SIX

How to Practice (But Not What You'd Think)

"And not only that, but we also glory in tribulations, knowing that tribulation produces perseverance; and perseverance, character; and character, hope. Now hope does not disappoint, because the love of God has been poured out in our hearts by the Holy Spirit who was given to us. For when we were still without strength, in due time Christ died for the ungodly. For scarcely for a righteous man will one die; yet perhaps for a good man someone would even dare to die. But God demonstrates His own love toward us, in that while we were still sinners, Christ died for us."

-Romans 5:3-8

"If you claim to be a follower of Jesus, but only believe what Jesus believes as long as He agrees with you, then you are not following Jesus, you are following yourself."[1]

–Red Pen Logic with Mr. B

If I could give a definition of the word "practice" I would say it is about finding the root problem, isolating it, and working it out. In practicing your music, find that problem area (such as a note or rhythm), isolate it to only practice that area, and dissect the measure or passage to find out what is causing the issue.

I was taught that if you can play the measure or passage three consecutive times without making a mistake after you work on that problem area, you have the passage pretty much secured. However, I always knew I had it down when I went from completely hating the passage to tolerating or even liking it. Once that passage was cleaned up, I would slowly add in the surrounding measures and play through the rest of the piece.

Once the measures are woven together smoothly with no breaks or hiccups, you have successfully practiced! Getting something down pat doesn't always happen overnight. It can be that way, but sometimes, you just sit and wrestle with it. Keep in mind, each day is different. A passage that is difficult to you one day may suddenly be easier to play the next day.

---

1. Barnett, Tim. "If You Claim to Be a Follower of Jesus, but Only Believe What Jesus Believes as Long as He Agrees with You, Then You Are Not Following Jesus, You Are Following Yourself." Red Pen Logic With Mr. B, July 3, 2023. Accessed July 3, 2023. https://www.facebook.com/redpenlogic.

Lately, my practice time looks like a type of "clearing the air" by removing my own thoughts and feelings as I come to the Lord in prayer before I ever play a note on my instrument. I've found I must clean up my thoughts and negative names before starting to practice.

You and I both know that if we entertain negative thoughts about our playing, we will not get very far. The same is true with our spiritual walk. What names are you calling yourself? The Lord will only call you by tender names — loved, cherished, forgiven. The enemy will call you names such as forgotten, abandoned, unlovable, or unworthy. We must stop allowing ourselves to be called what we fear or what was given to us as "truth." If it's not a loving name that you hear yourself being called, then you don't have to answer to it.

God may use a difficult season to refine you and make you more like Him, but you don't need to accept feelings or lies about your situation as to who you are. You must keep praying and using every ounce of mental willpower to give everything over to a loving God. First, you must be aware of what names you are responding to.

Because we know God isn't like men (Numbers 23:19), it is for that reason that we should cling to Him and accept His love for us and the names He tenderly calls us loved, forgiven, remembered, and cherished. In the Psalms, we are instructed to "play skillfully" (Psalm 33:3). We do our best and attain what we can, always aiming to better ourselves. I think about the Bible verse that says that "...perseverance gives way to character..." (Romans 5:3-5). When we struggle personally or musically, we wrestle well. We may not enjoy the difficulty, but we may yet come to appreciate and respect it.

"What you said really stuck with me," I spoke into the phone, between watching littles. "How can we know God the way y'all were raised? How can we see Him as loving while fearing Him?"[2] I asked Nancy.

"Well, Daddy taught us that God is loving but deserves our respect. With fathers not being as present as they were before in homes, it has made an effect on the family. Satan has always been after the family."

As Nancy and I talked over the course of the next hour or so, it became abundantly clear: when we stop putting people above God and not holding Him to the sins of those that hurt us, when we stop allowing Satan to have a "one-up" on us with pain man caused on us, we can begin to heal and see God as just, loving, and come to reverence H im.

Fathers are absent from homes more than ever, and people are living with so much pain that we become blinded and allow our hearts to harden. Feelings can be a liar, but I have concluded pain is a bigger platform Satan uses against us to steer our hearts away from God if we don't work through our pain and allow God to heal us.

I recently saw something from Cross Examined on Facebook that I thought made so much sense: "80% of a person's doubts do not stem from intellectual problems with Christianity, but rather from

2. Nancy, interview. September of 2021.

emotional doubt."[3] Furthermore, on a blog post on Cross Examined's website, the blogger, Chilton, explains that we can use Cognitive Behavioral Therapy (CBT) to help us. He argues that we can combat emotional doubt with CBT in three ways: "1. "Identify your lies. 2. Remove your lies by arguing against it and give reasons for your optimism. 3. Replace your lies with the truth of God's Word."

Sometimes we do need extra help working out things that are on our minds and hearts. Living in a first-world country, we do have the opportunity to seek counsel and help from others, but it's also easier to forget that this world is not perfect. Loved ones will eventually die, the unexpected will come and go. It's even more important to ground our minds in God's Word and remember this world is not our home.

The pain in our lives was never meant to turn us from God, but to Him instead. Perhaps one of the oldest questions we can ask is "If God is good, why does He allow bad things to happen to people?" God does not rejoice at wrong-doing, but due to The Fall of Man (when sin entered the world by the disobedience of Adam and Eve), we can see His great love to mankind.

Love will let something go, but control will induce force. God does not want us to follow Him out of force, but out of love. The utter ugliness someone inflicts upon another hurts God and helps us turn to Him and we can see His strength in our brokenness by Him upholding us and even changing us. God can use our story to help someone else. God cannot hurt us. We should want to turn to Someone perfect instead of imperfect people.

Remember that practicing your music and seeing the Lord as a just, loving Father result in your being a better musician overall. Give yourself a lot more grace. Then take a deep breath and relax. Set reasonable goals for your practice sessions and pursue them often. When you finish, breathe again, and give yourself even more grace.

Questions to Ponder:

• Where are you not choosing God? Where can you choose Him?

• If you value the opinions of others more than God, how can you begin to let that go and cling to God and His Word?

• What name(s) are you allowing yourself to be called? What names should you be responding to?

• What steps can you take to improve your practice time?

Amazing Grace
(John Newton, 1779)

1 Amazing grace (how sweet the sound)
that saved a wretch like me!
I once was lost, but now am found,
was blind, but now I see.

2 'Twas grace that taught my heart to fear,
and grace my fears relieved;
how precious did that grace appear
the hour I first believed!

3 Through many dangers, toils and snares
I have already come:
'tis grace has brought me safe thus far,
and grace will lead me home.

4 The Lord has promised good to me,
his word my hope secures;
he will my shield and portion be
as long as life endures.

5 Yes, when this flesh and heart shall fail,
and mortal life shall cease:
I shall possess, within the veil,
a life of joy and peace.

(Cont.)

6 The earth shall soon dissolve like snow,
the sun forbear to shine;
but God, who called me here below,
will be forever mine.

Hymnary.org. "Amazing Grace! (How Sweet the Sound)," n.d. https://hymnary.org/te xt/amazing_grace_how_sweet_the_sound. Accessed on July 1, 2023.

Hymn Study

1. Look up the backstory to this hymn. What strikes you most?

2. Now, look up the music to this hymn and play through it. It is necessary to understand lyrics and hear the music. Don't just play through it with no thought. Really think about what is being conveyed in this hymn.

3. Look up arrangements of this hymn by various artists on YouTube. Which arrangements do you gravitate to?

4. What do you feel like you gained from this hymn?

5. What do you perceive from this hymn about the Lord's character?

Thoughts/Notes/Prayers:

CHAPTER SEVEN

Playing with Excellence and How We Should Treat Classical Music

> "Sing to him a new song; play skillfully with a shout of joy."
>
> - Psalm 33:3

Rick and I had a blast accompanying our pianist on Sunday mornings at our church. He and his family befriended me and encouraged me in music during my high school and college years. With his bubbly personality and easy-going "it-is-what-it-is" attitude, we would enjoy cutting up a few minutes before we would play the prelude.

He would always leave out the chord every so often on guitar, if he didn't know or it was particularly hard. "Just gotta fake it, 'til you make it," he would joke and laugh freely. By the time the service came around, he settled into worship mode and focused on the hour to reverence the Lord.

Music theory, in my personal definition, is a guideline to make consonant, beautiful harmonies. I didn't see it that way in college and struggled in many of my music classes, if not them all; but a knowledgeable friend helped me better understand my one year of music theory classes and two years of aural skills classes.

There was so much to learn in a short time while I was in college; I don't know if it was how I was taught, my personal sensitivity, processing hard things, acute people-pleasing, or a little of all of it, but I lost that desire to practice anything classical. To be honest, I still don't practice a lot of Classical music. Hours spent practicing each day is just not where my heart is. In my current season of life, after one hour of practicing, I'm worn out. However, once I broke away from my perceived ideas of perfection, I started looking at music the way I believe God intends it as I invited Him into my practice time. Slowly, I began to appreciate the beauty of Classical music.

When I make practice about playing for Him and not for other people, I'm not as bitter about playing Classical music as I once was. I have my desire back to play with excellence, develop technical skills, review scales and etudes, and enjoy some Classical-style pieces.

The other day, I was surprised when I saw the composer's name, Felix Mendelssohn-Bartholdy, listed in an old hymn book of mine. I was certainly not expecting to see his name there. I often forget that some composers, such as Johann Sebastian Bach, have served the Lord through music. I don't know if it was the case with Mendelssohn too, but seeing his name made me think. How can we possibly see music differently if we have rigid and strict rules or mindsets about music?

What helped me to look at Classical music in a different facet is this question: What if music theory was Bach's way of giving back to the Lord? I ponder on the thought that, what if these guidelines and rules in music were created so others could understand and serve the Lord? What if music theory points us to God? There are simple progressions in hymns that stem from these rules, as well. Using the rules of music theory, I think men of similar or different beliefs took those guidelines and created their own music; adhering, stretching, or breaking these guidelines throughout the decades and centuries. Like language, music is constantly changing and adapting to the culture around its conception.

If you're struggling with understanding music theory or appreciating classical music, ask yourself how learning these concepts will shape your musical journey. Allow your mindset to shift as you consider this music as a means to glorify God. If you learn this new skill or enhance what you already know, you will be continuing to play with excellence.

Classical music does have a lot to teach us, both musically and historically, and it can help make us into better musicians. It helps us understand what happened in the past so we can shape our futures.

In addition to "being still" before God and asking Him to sit with you while you practice for His glory, here are a few other ideas to help with the mental load of practicing:

• Work carefully through those hardest sections. Find similar passages in etudes and practice those too.

• If you aren't into showy Classical pieces, try to find pieces that have a quiet strength about them but still showcase what you learned. One of my favorite pieces in this style is "Meditation de Thaïs" by Jules Massenet.

• If possible, try to pick pieces that you are interested in or certain eras of music history that pique your interest.

Practice is, more or less, picking apart a piece of music and learning as much about it as possible before weaving it back together. Get creative in your endeavors with learning these pieces. Maybe if we stop thinking of music theory as concrete rules for Classical music but rather an inspired design, it will make music-making for those who feel Classical music is difficult to play a bit easier and help us strive to serve the Lord, even in hard places.

We find that inspired design in hymns. Hymns are not musically complicated, but the rules J.S. Bach penned so long ago have stayed with music we hear today. How many people have the hymns inspired? How many churches have used these hymns over the last few centuries?

Questions to Ponder:

• How would your view on Classical music change if you saw it as a means to give glory to God?

• How can you sing or play Classical music so you can reflect the glory of God?

• What can you do to encourage someone else who is struggling with this genre of music?

Joyful, Joyful, We Adore Thee
(Henry Van Dyke, 1907)

1 Joyful, joyful, we adore You,

God of glory, Lord of love;

Hearts unfold like flow'rs before You,

Op'ning to the sun above.

Melt the clouds of sin and sadness;

Drive the dark of doubt away;

Giver of immortal gladness,

Fill us with the light of day!

2 All Your works with joy surround You,

Earth and heav'n reflect Your rays,

Stars and angels sing around You,

Center of unbroken praise;

Field and forest, vale and mountain,

Flow'ry meadow, flashing sea,

Chanting bird and flowing fountain

Praising You eternally!

3 Always giving and forgiving,

Ever blessing, ever blest,

Well-spring of the joy of living,

Ocean-depth of happy rest!

Loving Father, Christ our Brother,

Let Your light upon us shine;

Teach us how to love each other,

Lift us to the joy divine.

(Cont.)

4 Mortals, join the mighty chorus,
Which the morning stars began;
God's own love is reigning o'er us,
Joining people hand in hand.
Ever singing, march we onward,
Victors in the midst of strife;
Joyful music leads us sunward
In the triumph song of life.

Hymnary.org. "Joyful, Joyful, We Adore Thee," n.d. https://hymnary.org/text/joyful_
joyful_we_adore_thee. Accessed on July 2, 2023.

Hymn Study

1. Look up the backstory to this hymn. What strikes you most?

2. Now, look up the music to this hymn and play through it. It is necessary to understand lyrics and hear the music. Don't just play through it with no thought. Really think about what is being conveyed in this hymn.

3. Look up arrangements of this hymn by various artists on YouTube. Which arrangements do you gravitate to?

4. What do you feel like you gained from this hymn?

5. What do you perceive from this hymn about the Lord's character?

Thoughts/Notes/Prayers:

CHAPTER EIGHT

Playing as a Form of Expression

> "I will sing a new song to you, O God; on a harp of ten strings I will sing praises to You, The One who gives salvation to kings, Who delivers David His servant from the deadly sword. Rescue me and deliver me from the hand of foreigners, whose mouth speaks lying words, and whose right hand is a right hand of falsehood..."
>
> -Psalm 144:9-11

I met Kay after my husband and I were married. She had joined our church choir, and once it became know she also played piano, our music director asked her to play for the offertory or with Rick,

Tip (the bass guitarist), and me during the prelude. Kay had recently experienced a painful loss when her husband of a few decades passed away. It had been two or three years since he met the Lord, but she was still very much grieving.

Kay talked about how she would sit at home and play the Contemporary Christian song, "Still," as well as hymns and gospel songs because she considered it a devotion time with God. I could imagine the time she spent playing piano, perhaps even weeping, as she poured out her heart to God in song. She has since remarried, but I will never forget the pain that radiated from her and how she chose to spend her time with God in song. It made me wonder: What if we could pray to Him through song as we spend time with Him?

I have always liked the phrase found in Psalm 46:10, "Be still and know that I am God..." I like the emphasis on the word "still," but Kay posted the same Bible verse and emphasized the word "know." The Bible is multi-faceted, so we see new things as the Holy Spirit reveals them to us, wherever we are in life.

How many times have you started to pray, but couldn't do it? I don't mean a lack of words because of being in awe or having an empty heart before Him; I mean just not wanting to talk. It comes from a place of shying away from Him because you feel like He's upset with you or far away. What if your singing or playing severs that feeling and helps break down those emotional walls to speak to Him?

Hymns were written because of the relationship those lyricists had with God. When we, ourselves, are still, we know God better, and when we know Him better, we can help convey that tenderness and love of His voice and others through our music. The vibrato, fermatas, ritardando everything plays a part in how we express Who He is. Everything in our life is a result of Him and His handiwork in and through us.

How you interpret a musical passage is up to you. Has He been gentle and patient with you in a season of running from Him? Maybe reveal that in your interpretation with several crescendos and decrescendos. Keep the vibrato sweet and even, but with a touch of exaggeration. All these elements combine to make your experiences come alive through your music so others can hear it and glorify the Lord.

Questions to Ponder:

• Are you expressive when playing? If not, how can you improve? What specific steps can you take for this?

• How can you bring reverence to the Lord when playing with expressiveness?

• What techniques/skills can you use to help convey the meaning of the hymn?

• Have you ever tried humming your prayers in song to Him? If not, try it this week.

Come, Thou Fount of Every Blessing
(Author: Robert Robinson, 1758, Altered: Martin Madan, 1760)

1 Come, thou Fount of every blessing;
tune my heart to sing thy grace;
streams of mercy, never ceasing,
call for songs of loudest praise.
Teach me some melodious sonnet,
sung by flaming tongues above;
praise the mount! I'm fixed upon it,
mount of God's unchanging love!

2 Here I raise my Ebenezer;
hither by thy help I'm come;
and I hope, by thy good pleasure,
safely to arrive at home.
Jesus sought me when a stranger,
wandering from the fold of God;
he, to rescue me from danger,
interposed his precious blood.

(Cont.)

3 O to grace how great a debtor
daily I'm constrained to be!
Let that grace now, like a fetter,
bind my wandering heart to thee.
Prone to wander, Lord, I feel it,
prone to leave the God I love;
here's my heart; O take and seal it;
seal it for thy courts above.

Hymnary.org. "Come, Thou Fount of Every Blessing," n.d. https://hymnary.org/text
/come_thou_fount_of_every_blessing. Accessed on July 2, 2023

Hymn Study

1. Look up the backstory to this hymn. What strikes you most?

2. Now, look up the music to this hymn and play through it. It is necessary to understand lyrics and hear the music. Don't just play through it with no thought. Really think about what is being conveyed in this hymn.

3. Look up arrangements of this hymn by various artists on YouTube. Which arrangements do you gravitate to?

4. What do you feel like you gained from this hymn?

5. What do you perceive from this hymn about the Lord's character?

Thoughts/Notes/Prayers:

Chapter Nine

Musician Burnout

"Take My yoke upon you and learn from Me, for I am gentle and lowly in heart, and you will find rest for your souls."

-Matthew 11:29

Musician burnout is the lie of not doing enough. It looks like "not good enough," "imperfect," or just plain "nothing is right about any of it." Sometimes, burnout happens by overextending yourself for prolonged periods of time. That deep-set fatigue that seems to never go away, regardless of the amount of rest you get, could mean something more, especially when the burnout goes on for years at a time. The latter was my exact experience.

After sifting through all my emotions and finding ways to cope with some of the stressors of college, I felt unbelievably burned out after graduation. I rested for a few years, while diving into being a wife and mother and conducting private lessons. I tried practicing more often, but when I felt I wanted to play or when I would prepare for a wedding or church gig, I would always feel like "what's the point of playing?"

I needed a major shift of focus from outward to upward. I had to force myself to be still in every way and humble my heart before the Lord. I remembered the verses in Matthew 11:29-30 where Jesus said, "Take my yoke upon you, and learn from Me, for I am gentle and lowly in heart, and you will find rest for your souls. For My yoke is easy and My burden is light." That's exactly what I had to learn to do. I had to let go of the fermata of the chaos inside of me, and learn to rest in His presence.

If you find yourself facing musician burnout, invite God into the chaos into every part of your life in times of peace, seasons of grief, and even the mundane or monotonous days. This can be so hard to do sometimes! Every day, distractions in your life scream at you, vying for your attention. Yet, when you recognize this chaos storming around you and choose to stop and still your heart and mind, while getting adequate rest, you can work through burnout.

Sometimes this chaos can be influenced by, or a direct effect of, numerous hours of practice, certain high goals and stress, ideals of perfectionism, people-pleasing, or any combination of it all. If I'm being honest, I think there is a certain element in Classical music that is glamorized, glorified, and ultimately idolized that left me with a bad taste in my mouth for that genre. Even with this distaste, I have found I practice and play better (including Classical music) when I ultimately invite God into my mess and chaos.

If you are feeling the effects of burnout, there is hope! But it won't get better in its own time, without your surrendering it to God and allowing Him to sit with you amid the mess. As I said before, you don't have to be "perfect;" you just need to play with excellence. We will never be perfect on this side of Heaven, but we can do the best of our ability to practice and set reasonable goals for our musical growth, all the while, learning to rest in God. Invite Him into your practice sessions and open your heart as you play for Him, as if you are praying to Him.

Listening to and learning hymns are a source of freedom I found. By studying and playing through hymns, I learned to let go of my own perfectionism and give myself grace. I want to make sure that I practice and play the music correctly, especially in church, but when I'm at home, if I make a mistake, I can let that go a little easier. In church, it is my experience that most people will not openly critique us, even if the point of a critique is constructive. There are not many people who will notice a small mistake and if they do, they will not mention it. It's all about what God can do through you in music. We are a vessel using a vessel to make Him known. The Holy Spirit uses us to speak to others in ways we cannot see or fathom. We may never know how He uses us exactly, but He will!

Ephesians 2:10 states: "For we are His workmanship, created in Christ Jesus for good works, which God prepared beforehand that we should walk in them."

Musically and personally, it is so important to work to seize one moment at a time by giving it to God, walking through it with Him, and trying to not point a finger at Him if the road looks uncertain or not the way you planned. You don't get to look ahead at life as you can in music; you just have to trust that the day and moment you're living in isn't going to crumble under your feet because you aren't in control. Sometimes, being still is so hard and painful to do, but it's how to get through what you can't get through on your own.

Questions to Ponder:

• Have you been experiencing musical burnout? If so, where is the burnout stemming from? Perfectionism? Too much practicing? People-pleasing? Something else?

• How might you surrender those areas to the Lord?

• What is your next step, no matter how small?

• Answer honestly: Do you need to seek professional help to deal with burnout? (Important note: I believe the Lord sometimes leads us to others to help us heal from our deep-seated burnout and depression. Do not feel any shame in seeking out professional help if you find yourself in a dark place emotionally, spiritually, or physically.)

Great is Thy Faithfulness
(Thomas O. Chisholm, 1923)

1 Great is Thy faithfulness, O God my Father;
there is no shadow of turning with Thee;
Thou changest not, Thy compassions, they fail not;
as Thou hast been Thou forever wilt be.

Refrain:
Great is Thy faithfulness!
Great is Thy faithfulness!
Morning by morning new mercies I see;
all I have needed Thy hand hath provided:
great is Thy faithfulness, Lord, unto me!

2 Summer and winter, and springtime and harvest;
sun, moon, and stars in their courses above
join with all nature in manifold witness
to Thy great faithfulness, mercy, and love. [Refrain]

3 Pardon for sin and a peace that endureth,
Thine own dear presence to cheer and to guide;
strength for today and bright hope for tomorrow:
blessings all mine, with ten thousand beside! [Refrain]

Hymnary.org. "Great Is Thy Faithfulness," n.d. https://hymnary.org/text/great_is_thy
_faithfulness_o_god_my_fathe. Accessed on July 3, 2023

Hymn Study

1. Look up the backstory to this hymn. What strikes you most?

2. Now, look up the music to this hymn and play through it. It is necessary to understand lyrics and hear the music. Don't just play through it with no thought. Really think about what is being conveyed in this hymn.

3. Look up arrangements of this hymn by various artists on YouTube. Which arrangements do you gravitate to?

4. What do you feel like you gained from this hymn?

5. What do you perceive from this hymn about the Lord's character?

Thoughts/Notes/Prayers:

CHAPTER TEN

Musician Depression

"When you pass through the waters, I will be with you; and through the rivers, they shall not overflow you. When you walk through the fire, you shall not be burned, nor shall the flame scorch you."

-Isaiah 43:2

The summer before my junior year of college, I felt an ocean of sadness I had not felt before. It took time and perspective to recognize the tsunami I felt was due to grief over lost time with my loved one, unresolved trauma, and a lot of stress from school. I felt some big pressures with practicing and schoolwork, and a lack of sleep didn't help any of this. It was a dark time. The exhaustion and unresolved trauma led me to feelings of loneliness, anger, and an inability to trust people.

Practicing my music was hard. I didn't want to do it. It physically hurt to practice, and it was draining and not enjoyable in the least. I felt I had few people who truly knew my heart. You really do learn who your friends are during a time like that. What eventually helped me navigate my way through this season was being with family and the few friends who deeply knew me. Being uplifted by these people helped me keep my sole identity from being only about school and music.

When I needed to perform in a peer-based constructive criticism class, I would pray and ask God to take control and help me play for Him, do my best while playing after I had practiced my hardest, and leave the rest up to God. With constructive criticism, I would listen, seek to understand, and not take anything too personally after doing all I could possibly do to prepare my music. Once I started doing this, the burden of studying music got easier. I found the right medication, met my future husband, and got through my senior year with a successful senior recital behind me. I married my husband seven months after graduation, and our family grew soon after we married.

If you find yourself in a similar place, where studying music has become a heavy burden you're struggling to carry, I hope these thoughts help:

◦ Find that root that is causing so much pain, and pluck it out so there is less stress on you.

◦ Let things go and do the best you can. You can't think about how you don't measure up to someone else's expectations.

◦ Set small, reasonable goals to achieve. Celebrate when you achieve them.

◦ Realize that life happens, and you have little control over it. Each season brings its own challenges, and needs grace for how much time you practice. Remember: Quality over quantity, every time.

◦ You are not a machine. You must REST! Rest in the Lord, rest in the truth found in His Word and hymns, and give yourself grace.

These days, I've been off medication for several years and worked through so much of those ugly lies I once believed. When practicing my music, what helps me is to sit and be still before I begin.

I challenge you to invite God into the chaos of your life. In prayer, tell Him what's bothering you, and cry in His presence if you need to. Then dry your tears, pick up your instrument, and play what you feel you can, to the best of your ability. Playing for Him looks like using your instrument (or voice) as a prayer to Him, even if you aren't playing a hymn. If you are directing your music to Him and for Him, you are playing for Him. Take life one step, one moment at a time. Your best is all you can do. Seasons come and go outside of your control. Why not surrender it all to the One Who is in control?

Questions to Ponder:

• What reasonable goals can you create in your personal and music life?

• Are you giving yourself grace?

• Is there anything you haven't worked through? If so, how might you do that? What are your next steps?

My Hope is Built on Nothing Less
(Edward Mote, 1834)

1 My hope is built on nothing less
than Jesus' blood and righteousness;
I dare not trust the sweetest frame,
but wholly lean on Jesus' name.

Refrain:
On Christ, the solid Rock, I stand:
all other ground is sinking sand;
all other ground is sinking sand.

2 When darkness veils his lovely face,
I rest on his unchanging grace;
in every high and stormy gale,
my anchor holds within the veil. [Refrain]

3 His oath, his covenant, his blood,
support me in the whelming flood;
when all around my soul gives way,
he then is all my hope and stay. [Refrain]

4 When he shall come with trumpet sound,
O may I then in him be found:
dressed in his righteousness alone,
faultless to stand before the throne. [Refrain]

Hymnary.org. "My Hope Is Built on Nothing Less," n.d. https://hymnary.org/text/m
y_hope_is_built_on_nothing_less.Accessed on July 5, 2023.

Hymn Study

1. Look up the backstory to this hymn. What strikes you most?

2. Now, look up the music to this hymn and play through it. It is necessary to understand lyrics and hear the music. Don't just play through it with no thought. Really think about what is being conveyed in this hymn.

3. Look up arrangements of this hymn by various artists on YouTube. Which arrangements do you gravitate to?

4. What do you feel like you gained from this hymn?

5. What do you perceive from this hymn about the Lord's character?

Thoughts/Notes/Prayers:

CHAPTER ELEVEN

Church Music

"I will remember the works of the Lord; surely I will remember Your wonders of old. I will also meditate on all Your work and talk of all Your deeds."

-Psalm 77:11-12

When my family started attending my mom's home church, my brother and I were baptized there, having accepted the Lord some time before. Going to our church was the first time we had really started attending church regularly, and there I discovered a new desire: I wanted to serve God through music. I prayed about it, and God made a way for me to serve right in my church. Church members found out I played violin and asked me to play at a Christmas evening service; the rest is history. God put people in my life who also served the Lord through church music, and I've seen one door opened after another. One friend, Kathy, started an ensemble at church and mentored and encouraged me. She was doing what God called her to do starting church orchestras. Today, she still plays in the orchestras she starts at local churches.

The Lord is looking for those who are willing to be used by Him through our music. In whatever role He puts us in we need to continue to "...make a joyful noise unto the Lord" (Psalm 100:1). If we are musicians, let those who lead, lead and those who follow, follow, each always esteeming "...others higher than himself" (Philippians 2:3).

Even if you are playing behind an organ (I have always preferred growing up to hide while playing), those who need to hear your interpretation or musical thumbprint can be impacted for the better. I know when the Lord is invited, music becomes a ministry. Whatever the Lord brings us to, He can use it to change us personally and spiritually. Whatever He uses to shape us, can later be used to help others who are going through a difficult time of refinement.

Playing music with others in a church setting can be emotionally-binding. After I perform with someone, I usually feel closer to them, even if we aren't friends. Performing music with others causes serotonin to be released, but we should not substitute that feeling for our relationship with God. We don't have to get caught up in the middle of a concert to be connected to God, yet so many do.

It seems to me, some Contemporary Christian music requires that we look within and then up to God to assert our own thoughts on how He views our happiness, thus making the song about how we feel after we sing about said happiness. However, I have found that the promises that are in some of the Contemporary music make more sense after studying the hymns, seeing the Lord for Who He is, and accepting His character. Hymns don't talk about the happiness and feel-good life God supposedly wants for us. They don't give an emotional "high" like some Contemporary Christian songs. Hymns have us look first to God, then within ourselves. They don't promise it will all be okay; rather, they say God will help us make it through whatever we may face.

I enjoy most Contemporary Christian songs, but many are like the potatoes or starches on a dinner plate or sprinkles on top of a cupcake. They remind us of God and get our thoughts focused on Him, but hymns touch you to the core because of their rich Theology.

Look at David's songs in the book of the Psalms. He presents his very real, raw emotions and then counters them by exclaiming how great and mighty Jehovah is. He looks to God, and that changes everything. Even during the time of ancient Israelite music, they always turned back to worship and thank God for what He was going to do because of their faith in Him. So perhaps our own trials bring about new songs borne in us. I wonder if the Lord gives musicians (or any artist) certain trials to endure so that we can tell others through song how to get through those trials by always looking to the Lord.

We best serve the Lord in church music when we make it about Him and work together to make it all one accord. We should encourage those who are looking to serve and make room for them in the service, even if they aren't technically "good." So long as they have a heart for the Lord and have a musically legible melody line with a servant's heart, the Lord still uses it (which is something I love!).

For the musicians who may play harmony lines or be the "backup" elsewhere, we should serve joyfully, knowing that God uses harmonies just as much as he does melodies. We should encourage those beneath us and those above us. For those who are leaders of any kind, we should strive to include everyone who wants to serve, encourage them, receive constructive criticism with consideration, and help everyone else be reminded the music is about the Lord, not ourselves. Even the leader must submit to a higher authority while keeping in mind the admonition from Romans 12:3 "not to think of himself more highly than he ought to think." We should remember 1 Corinthians 12:18-20, stating "But now God has set the members, each one of them, in the body just as He pleased. And if they were all one member, where would the body be? But now indeed there are many members, yet one body."

You and your special gift of music have a place in the Body of Christ.

Questions to Ponder:

• Do you feel a sense of serving others in some area of ministry (such as church music)? If so, what might you need to do to get started on this path?

• How should people treat other musicians as they play in church?

• Have you played in a church setting but stepped back? What would help get you back into serving musically? Is this something you need the Lord to help you overcome? If so, what are your next steps?

Are You Washed in the Blood
(E. A. Hoffman, 1878)

1 Have you been to Jesus for the cleansing power?
Are you washed in the blood of the Lamb?
Are you fully trusting in His grace this hour?
Are you washed in the blood of the Lamb?

Chorus:
Are you washed in the blood,
In the soul cleansing blood of the Lamb?
Are your garments spotless?
Are they white as snow?
Are you washed in the blood of the Lamb?

2 Are you walking daily by the Savior's side?
Are you washed in the blood of the Lamb?
Do you rest each moment in the Crucified?
Are you washed in the blood of the Lamb? [Chorus]

3 When the Bridegroom cometh will your robes be white?
Are you washed in the blood of the Lamb?
Will your soul be ready for the mansions bright,
And be washed in the blood of the Lamb? [Chorus]

(Cont.)

4 Lay aside the garments that are stained with sin,

And be washed in the blood of the Lamb;

There's a fountain flowing for the soul unclean,

O be washed in the blood of the Lamb! [Chorus]

Hymnary.org. "Are You Washed in the Blood?," n.d. https://hymnary.org/text/have_y ou_been_to_jesus_for_the_cleansing. Accessed on July 5, 2023.

Hymn Study

1. Look up the backstory to this hymn. What strikes you most?

2. Now, look up the music to this hymn and play through it. It is necessary to understand lyrics and hear the music. Don't just play through it with no thought. Really think about what is being conveyed in this hymn.

3. Look up arrangements of this hymn by various artists on YouTube. Which arrangements do you gravitate to?

4. What do you feel like you gained from this hymn?

5. What do you perceive from this hymn about the Lord's character?

Thoughts/Notes/Prayers:

CHAPTER TWELVE

The Lie of Living Less Than

"Can a woman forget her nursing child, And not have compassion on the son of her womb? Surely they may forget, Yet I will not forget you. See, I have inscribed you on the palms of My hands; Your walls are continually before Me."

-Isaiah 49:15-16

There are many people walking around today who live as if they are less than - less than their neighbors, friends, other musicians, and less than deserving of the care and sight of God. Living under these presumptions and wrong ideals we were taught causes more harm than good. They keep us from living full lives, inadvertently driving away potential friends, and keeping us from performing as we would in the secret practice rooms of our lives. So many people walk around not knowing that they are stuck in these thought patterns, but eventually they will get to a point where they have to fight it, because if they don't, they will be perpetually stuck.

It is tempting to think God has forgotten you or that you are less than someone else, especially if you have had someone disappear from your life. It leaves the scars of abandonment which can be internalized and personalized. At least, that is what happened for me. I had to come to a point where I decided it was time to gird myself and fight back against those thoughts that God would treat me the same as the person who mentally left me.

A great article from The National Association for Christian Recovery explains how we can heal from childhood trauma with the help of the Lord. Juanita Ryan says that the healing process is not linear, nor does it have a quick processing time, but it is possible with help from loved ones and God.[1] She goes on to say the following and provides the helpful table below:

> "We may fear that God is like the adults who hurt us, or like the adults who did not protect us. We may fear that God is disappointed with us, has forgotten us, or is disgusted with us. Our deepest healing will be to discover that God is none of these things. God is revealed to us as 'the Father of compassion and the God of all comfort,' who 'daily bears our burdens.'

---

1. The National Association for Christian Recovery. "Recovery from Childhood Trauma," December 15, 2017. https://www.nacr.org/abusecenter/recovery-from-childhood-trauma-2. Accessed on July 7, 2023.

God is eager to show us directly and personally how deeply loved and valued we each are. Our part is to risk inviting God to comfort us, to reveal love to us, and to open our minds and hearts to receive all the gifts of grace we need in order to fully heal [. . .] With the continued help of God and others, we become more aware, acknowledge more, and integrate more fully. And then, again, with help, we see more, accept more and embrace more. This cycle continues until we deeply embrace our experience and ourselves and know ourselves embraced."

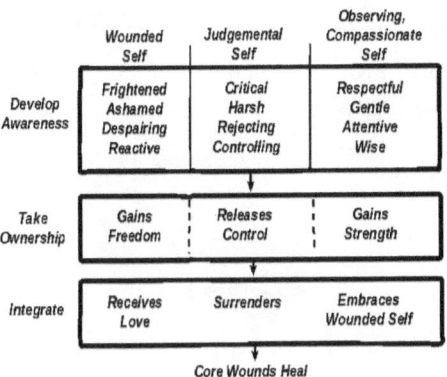

	Wounded Self	Judgemental Self	Observing, Compassionate Self
Develop Awareness	Frightened Ashamed Despairing Reactive	Critical Harsh Rejecting Controlling	Respectful Gentle Attentive Wise
Take Ownership	Gains Freedom	Releases Control	Gains Strength
Integrate	Receives Love	Surrenders	Embraces Wounded Self

Core Wounds Heal

The most painful core wound I unknowingly carried into adulthood was healed. My deep-seated rejection had told me that I was already rejected by friends, classmates, and random people in grocery stores. I once believed that no matter what I said or did, I would never be accepted. This led me to isolate myself and put up a wall around myself. I also found it hard to embrace love I was shown. I reasoned that since I had experienced rejection by others, that I must be unlovable. The Lord sent special people into my life who saw past my walls and touched my literal heart (like my sweet husband), but I still could not move past the deep-set pain. The pain grew so intense in my heart that I would cry myself to sleep. The hurt eventually became more and more frequent and painful until I finally cried out to God in a desperate prayer: "Please help me! Please take this away from me. I don't want it anymore! Please heal me!"

When I cried to Him from the depths of my heart, He heard me, immediately stopped my crying, and took away the pain that had cut me to my core. I walked around elated for days. In His love and compassion, He healed me of things I could not heal on my own. He sees and cares! I am living proof that core wounds can be healed.

Do you remember when I spoke on the abandonment tendencies I felt in college? I had a drive to please and do things "just right" musically, academically, and relationally. I was afraid that I would not be seen, and I eventually just resolved to be okay with not being truly seen. I felt safer this way because if I didn't let anyone get close to me, I reasoned I wouldn't get hurt if they left.

In the Lord's compassion and love for me, He put it on an associate pastor's heart to preach on abandonment and feelings. On Mt. Gallagher Baptist Church's YouTube channel, Pastor Jacob quoted Hebrews 12:1-3:

> "Therefore we also, since we are surrounded by so great a cloud of witnesses, let us lay aside every weight, and the sin which so easily ensnares us, and let us run with endurance the race that is set before us, looking unto Jesus, the author and finisher of our faith, who for the joy that was set before Him endured the cross, despising the shame, and has sat down at the right hand of the throne of God. For consider Him who endured such hostility from sinners against Himself, lest you become weary and discouraged in your soul s."[2]

Pastor Jacob made a point that we are to lay aside everything that holds us back from running our race, which includes abandonment, anxiety, and depression. The only way we can combat abandonment, he goes on to say, is by abandoning abandonment. We are to keep our minds fixed on God and daily give our thorns to Him. Jacob

---

2. Mt. Gallagher Baptist Church, Jacob Schultz, Guest Speaker, 31:26-56:34, February 25, 2024, https://www.youtube.com/watch?v=sDXpC8SYk1Y.

stated that Satan wants us to remain stagnant in our faith and not really move forward or enjoy where we are. We carry weights, such as abandonment and trauma, that keep us from "experiencing the freedom God has for you" and we must "...make the decision to leave them." Jacob further explains these weights "keep you where you are and keep you looking back at your past." Second to the Gospel, I've never heard anything truer. God's compassion for you and me is so clearly laid out. I had never thought of Hebrews 12:1-2 in such a way before. This leads to another question: What is compassion?

Baker's Evangelical Dictionary of Biblical Theology gives us a clear definition of compassion, found in the Bible:

> The Hebrew (hamal [l;m'j], rachuwm [Wj;r]) and Greek (splanchnisomai [splagcNIVzomai]) words sometimes translated as "compassion" also bear a broader meaning such as "to show pity, " "to love, " and "to show mercy." Other near synonyms for compassion in English are "to be loved by, " "to show concern for, " "to be tenderhearted, " and "to act kindly."[3]

There are many instances in the Bible where we see the compassion and tenderness of the Lord. For example:

• Lamentations 3:22-23: "Through the Lord's mercies we are not consumed, Because His compassions fail not. They are new every morning; Great is Your faithfulness."

---

3. Engelhart, David H. Bible Study Tools. "Compassion - Bible Definition and Scripture References," n.d. https://www.biblestudytools.com/dictionary/compassion/. Accessed on February 16, 2024.

• Psalm 86:15: "But You, O Lord, are a God full of compassion, and gracious, Longsuffering and abundant in mercy and truth."

• Psalm 103:13: "As a father pities his children, So the Lord pities those who fear Him."

• Psalm 116:5: "Gracious is the Lord, and righteous; Yes, our God is merciful."

• Psalm 145:8-9: "The Lord is gracious and full of compassion, Slow to anger and great in mercy. The Lord is good to all, And His tender mercies are over all His works."

• John 11:32-36: "Then, when Mary came where Jesus was, and saw Him, she fell down at His feet, saying to Him, 'Lord, if You had been here, my brother would not have died.' Therefore, when Jesus saw her weeping, and the Jews who came with her weeping, He groaned in the spirit and was troubled. And He said, 'Where have you laid him?' They said to Him, 'Lord, come and see.' Jesus wept. Then the Jews said, 'See how He loved him!'"

• Romans 5:8: "But God demonstrates His own love toward us, in that while we were still sinners, Christ died for us."

• Ephesians 2:4-10: "But God, who is rich in mercy, because of His great love with which He loved us, even when we were dead in trespasses, made us alive together with Christ (by grace you have been saved), and raised us up together, and made us sit together in the heavenly places in Christ Jesus, that in the ages to come He might show the exceeding riches of His grace in His kindness toward us in Christ Jesus. For by grace you have been saved through faith, and that not of yourselves; it is the gift of God, not of works, lest anyone should boast. For we are His workmanship, created in Christ Jesus for good works, which God prepared beforehand that we should walk in them."

• 1 John 4:7-10: "Beloved, let us love one another, for love is of God; and everyone who loves is born of God and knows God. He who does not love does not know God, for God is love. In this the love of God was manifested toward us, that God has sent His only begotten Son into the world, that we might live through Him. In this is love, not that we loved God, but that He loved us and sent His Son to be the propitiation for our sins."

• 1 John 4:19: "We love Him because He first loved us."

It's always helpful to learn more about God's perfect, infallible love. From Alisa Childers and Tim Barnett's book, The Deconstruction of Christianity, we find that "Biblically speaking the definition of love begins with the nature and character of God."[4] Barnett and Childers give the example of the passage from 1 Corinthians 13 on love and make it a point to add that the "true definition of love does not celebrate harmful or sinful things." God cannot sin or lie (see Numbers 23:19). In other words, we can only begin to truly know God when we see the distinction between man and God.

Once you begin to see God's love at work in your life, you can choose to focus on positive thoughts as you leave your life of "less than" behind. In Chapter 16 of Jennie Allen's book Dangerous Thinking, she speaks about Peter walking to Jesus on the water. Allen states the following:

> "When we choose to shift our thoughts that distract and fix our minds on Him, everything shifts . . . Jesus' face is the object of focus. When we focus on Him everything else becomes strangely dim."

---

4. Alisa Childers and Tim Barnett, The Deconstruction of Christianity: What It Is, Why It's Destructive, and How to Respond. Audiobook. (Tyndale Elevate, 2024). Chapter 3: Rerun. Accessed on February 19, 2024.

She goes on to say that ". . . our thoughts dictate our beliefs, which dictate our actions, which form our habits, which compose the sum of our lives." After listening to this chapter, my main takeaway is this: we must flood our minds with His Word, songs, prayers. We are to "pray without ceasing" (1 Thessalonians 5:17). That is how we can be more like our grandparents' generation, by flooding our thoughts with Him.

Your life is about Him! In music, you are gifted with a musical thumbprint that only you possess. God can use your voice and timbre to reach those who need to hear it. It's nothing that you can do on your own, but something only He can do because of Who He is and how He loves you. You are loved, seen, and heard. The Creator of the Universe wants your surrender so you can be free!

Questions to Ponder:

• What other verses can you find about the compassion and tenderness of the Lord?

• Do you struggle with seeing Him as kind and loving? Why or why not?

• What can help you see Him as good?

Standing on the Promises
(Russel Kelso Carter, 1886)

1 Standing on the promises of Christ, my King,

Through eternal ages let his praises ring;

Glory in the highest, I will shout and sing,

Standing on the promises of God.

Refrain:

Standing, standing,

Standing on the promises of God, my Savior;

Standing, standing,

I'm standing on the promises of God.

2 Standing on the promises that cannot fail.

When the howling storms of doubt and fear assail,

By the living Word of God I shall prevail,

Standing on the promises of God. [Refrain]

3 Standing on the promises of Christ, the Lord,

Bound to him eternally by love's strong cord,

Overcoming daily with the Spirit's sword,

Standing on the promises of God. [Refrain]

4 Standing on the promises I cannot fall,

List'ning ev'ry moment to the Spirit's call,

Resting in my Savior as my all in all,

Standing on the promises of God. [Refrain]

Hymnary.org. "Standing on the Promises," n.d. https://hymnary.org/text/standing_on_the_promises_of_christ_my_ki. Accessed on July 5, 2023.

Hymn Study

1. Look up the backstory to this hymn. What strikes you most?

2. Now, look up the music to this hymn and play through it. It is necessary to understand lyrics and hear the music. Don't just play through it with no thought. Really think about what is being conveyed in this hymn.

3. Look up arrangements of this hymn by various artists on YouTube. Which arrangements do you gravitate to?

4. What do you feel like you gained from this hymn?

5. What do you perceive from this hymn about the Lord's character?

Thoughts/Notes/Prayers:

CHAPTER THIRTEEN

Performance Anxiety

"Therefore, whether you eat or drink, or whatever you do, do all to the glory of God."

-1 Corinthians 10:31

"The aim and final result of all music should be none other than the glory of God and the refreshment of the soul."

-J.S. Bach

I like the idea of performing, but the act of doing so can be difficult for me. I feel as if I open myself up and my soul is naked before everyone. My right bow hand will shake, and my left wrist will get tense and inflexible. My intonation goes south and everything I seemingly worked for goes down the drain. I don't really get to properly showcase all I worked so hard on in the practice room, but then again, it wasn't mine to completely claim. My hard work and dedication are admirable, but the ability and interpretation of the music came from the Lord, the ultimate Giver of tones and timbres.

I play my best music in church because I don't feel like there is a huge weight or pressure to be "perfect". There have been a few times I can think of where I let go of my need to "perform" or "wear a mask" musically-speaking. One instance was when I was in a performance class in college, and I had just deleted a lot of stress from my life. I was so elated that I didn't think hard about performing. I didn't worry or overthink things, I just simply let go and didn't care about the musical mask (act of performing a piece) that came across. It was what it was.

Perhaps performance anxiety also boils down to feeling like we need to put on a show for the listener. We try to tailor it to the person receiving it, but we can't really do that. Each person has their own musical thumbprint and also their own thoughts about how something should be played, even within the bounds of a technical definition of a classical piece, such as Baroque music with no vibrato. Maybe performance anxiety also is the outward expression of all our other personal anxieties that we carry around. We shouldn't walk on eggshells, so to speak, when we play. We should do things as they're written or intended, but not live in fear that we will be musically condemned if we don't perform as any listener thinks we ought.

While musicians must have an element of "fake it 'til you make it" in performing, you can't get caught up in the same pattern with every-day life. You can't "fake it 'til you make it" with your pains and hurts. Pain stays and only gets worse if you don't deal with what's causing it. Music that truly touches you deep down and brings tears to your eyes can bring you to a place of surrendering your pain to the Lord. Please understand I am not saying that music should always evoke emotions, but sometimes it does. The Lord can use music to touch the deepest part of your heart and give you a doorway to surrender those hurts and pains more easily to Him.

In Psalm 139:13-18, we find that God made who we are, saw us before we were born, and numbered our days. Sometimes we can buy into the lie perpetuated by the world that something is inherently wrong with our core being. We must come to a place where we surrender that lie to God. This looks like crying out to Him from the depths of our pain, lowering all our walls to Him that He already sees through, and praying something like the following:

> "Here I am, Lord, bringing all my shame to you. I don't want to feel this way about myself anymore. It's not who you made me to be, but I can't get past it on my own. Please take me, heal me, and help me live totally devoted to You. Thank You, God. In Jesus' Name I pray, Amen."

When I prayed a similar prayer to the one above, I felt the most comfortable with who God created me to be for the first time in a long time. No more overthinking, no more responding to names I am not, no more shame I wrongfully carried because of past hurts, no more hiding who I am. My burden was gone, and I was free. You can be free too. All He ever wanted was our complete and total surrender of everything.

In college, I learned several coping skills for my performance anxiety, letting the result of my practicing and playing my best fall back on God, and using the outcome for His glory. I learned to clench my fists and then release them to help calm the shaking. I began playing each piece of music for God, without aiming to please anyone else.

Despite doing these things over the years, I still respond anxiously to performing, but it has gotten easier over the years as I've realized that my sense of overthinking and past hurts and pains have likely ruled in places I didn't see. Making music about personal fun and enjoyment and thinking it is adding to someone else's life has made performing much less stressful for me. Also, just practicing really does make things easier over time.

My senior recital was no walk in the park. The years leading up to it were treacherous on my mind and heart as I prepared. One thing that helped me get warmed up for my recital was playing the hymn, "Blessed Assurance." It took my mind off everything outward and lifted my thoughts upward. I took a great step in the right direction with my recital, and that performance changed my outlook from myself and others and placed it back on the Lord where it always belonged. I accredit that God uses the season and walk of the composer or lyricist to bring about the building of His Kingdom in subtle, but mighty ways. He can take ordinary people and use them to shed the light of His love, glory, and His heart to all generations, even if they don't play an instrument.

I recently had a lightbulb moment. Before playing at my grandma-in-law's funeral, those insecurities, fears, and jitters were just churning in my body, when suddenly, I looked out to the gathering and realized that it really does not matter who my audience is or how many are in it. All that truly matters in the end, is playing for the Lord and accepting His love for me because those two things change so much.

One of the bravest things we can do is to let God work through our weaknesses, even our performing anxieties. You can surrender your hurts and pains. He will show up and show Himself true to you. This is how you exchange your performance anxiety for a steadfast confidence in the Lord.

Questions to Ponder:

• What coping skills do you have for performance anxiety?

• Is it easy for you to perform? Why or why not? Either way, is there anything you can do to get better?

• What light-bulb moment(s) have you had with performing?

• Are there any areas in your life today that need surrendering? When will you do that?

Blessed Assurance
(Fanny Crosby, 1873)

1 Blessed assurance, Jesus is mine!
Oh, what a foretaste of glory divine!
Heir of salvation, purchase of God,
born of his Spirit, washed in his blood.

Refrain:
This is my story, this is my song,
praising my Savior all the day long.
This is my story, this is my song,
praising my Savior all the day long.

2 Perfect communion, perfect delight,
visions of rapture now burst on my sight.
Angels descending bring from above
echoes of mercy, whispers of love. [Refrain]

3 Perfect submission, all is at rest.
I in my Savior am happy and bless'd,
watching and waiting, looking above,
filled with his goodness, lost in his love. [Refrain]

Hymnary.org. "Blessed Assurance," n.d. https://hymnary.org/text/blessed_assurance _jesus_is_mine. Accessed on July 6, 2023.

Hymn Study

1. Look up the backstory to this hymn. What strikes you most?

2. Now, look up the music to this hymn and play through it. It is necessary to understand lyrics and hear the music. Don't just play through it with no thought. Really think about what is being conveyed in this hymn.

3. Look up arrangements of this hymn by various artists on YouTube. Which arrangements do you gravitate to?

4. What do you feel like you gained from this hymn?

5. What do you perceive from this hymn about the Lord's character?

Thoughts/Notes/Prayers:

CHAPTER FOURTEEN

The Weight of Hymns in Our World Today

"Sometimes, being different feels a lot like being alone. But with that being said, being true to that and being true to my standards and my way of doing things in my art and my music, everything that has made me feel very different... in the end, it has made me the happiest."

- Lindsey Stirling

"All I used to hear was squawk, squawk, squawk," Granny told a family friend one day when referring to my practicing. "But, she has gotten pretty good," she added with a proud smile. I sheepishly smiled back.

"She has done well; I bet you are proud, Nancy," Granny's friend replied. I glowed knowing Granny was proud of me.

That moment happened fourteen years ago when I was staying the night with Granny and Papa. It feels like a lifetime ago.

March of 2022 found me playing her favorite hymn, "Amazing Grace" at her funeral. I always loved my Granny very much, but it wasn't until her death that I realized just how much of an impact she left on me. She didn't play any instruments or sing herself, but she did love me and everyone else she met with all her heart. She never met a stranger. Most importantly, she loved the Lord and was a wonderful example of how we should constantly seek Him and have our hearts ever bent before Him.

Our grandparents' generation often came to the Lord in prayer. They also wrote songs about Him so when they weren't praying or reading their Bibles, they were singing. They surrendered their weights to Him and did their best to keep God as their upmost focus.

I believe hymns show loving faith in action from humans to our God. Hymns are an act of worship in the whole process of writing, composing, listening, singing, and playing. They are an ongoing act of surrender, based on our relationship of being fully known and loved by God. This is something Lysa TerKeurst talks about, stating:

> "God doesn't want us to stay stuck in our places of blame and hurt. He wants to heal us and help us move forward. I don't know what from your past still causes you pain today, friend. But I do know that the only thing that will stop the desperation, the uncertainties, the insecurities, is to realize those people who unfairly rejected us were putting their own hurt on display much more than making a defining statement about

us...What they did doesn't mean you only deserve scraps of love from others. You are fully known and fully loved by a God whose greatest joy is to be with you."34

God wants you to surrender your pain to Him daily. It was never yours to keep, and it doesn't have to define you. God makes you whole and gives you a new life. Yes, it's a difficult process, but it is absolutely, 100% necessary. When you give up your pain, it touches the heart of God. This is how it should be when we are playing any genre of music. It should be an act of love to God, surrendering all of us to Him.

Granny's old red barn I always admired. She and Papa had cows and this was one of my favorite places on the property.

Barnett and Childers explain the current state of our individualistic culture in The Deconstruction of Christianity that hits the nail on the head:

> "Today, we live in a culture where human beings are defined by their individual, inner feelings and desires. We are encouraged to live in a way that lines up with those feelings and desires, which becomes our ultimate authority. Anything that challenges that notion is considered to be oppressive, especially Bible verses that contradict your own personal expression."35

It is astonishing we have come to this point in society. I think one of the biggest things that separates our generation from generations of the past is our inability to be still and trust in our Savior. We fear that God will be like the ones who caused our broken views of humans. We put our trust in people and place them on a pedestal above God and then blame Him when others hurt us. We do not have a deep, Biblical relationship with God through Jesus. We cannot put all our focus on Him because we don't trust Him. We've accepted "brokenness" as our name instead of adopting His true names for us loved, chosen, remembered, cherished, and valuable. We do not see God as an approachable, loving Father to the fatherless. We cannot accept His love to us or accept the love others have for us. Instead, we view God as distant. If we don't see the truth of Who God is, will we trust Him, spend time with Him, or talk to Him throughout the day? No, because our relationship is broken.

If we cannot allow ourselves to be loved because we feel there is something unlovable about us, we cannot fully walk free of past shadows and enjoy the life we have and find joy in the small things everyday. Love is scary, but it is a necessary human need and important to accept that love is freely given, even if we think undeserving or falsely believe something is deeply wrong with us. If we can embrace some people we are close to, show us love and see in the everyday mundane how God loves us deeply and lean into those, we can begin living our life richly.

It's one thing to accept Jesus as Lord and Savior and another to surrender your hurts to Him, but it's entirely something beautiful all on its own when we step into who God calls us: cherished, loved, not forsaken, not forgotten and to live in those new names. Live your life to the fullest in Him, never forsaking those names and "walk worthy of your calling" (Ephesians 4:1). From here, you truly can experience Chords of Hope. The good news is that we can find spiritual healing through worship!

Worshiping with hymns reminds me to not allow my feelings to dictate my life. I no longer view God as the angry and distant God I perceived Him to be growing up. When I started seeing God as someone who is kind and wants to have a relationship with us through the hymns, my spiritual eyes were opened. I gradually let down some of my walls and came to Him. When I wanted to keep my walls up, I laid out my heart and depended on Him to be my rock.

I spent several years trying to heal myself of the things from childhood I allowed to define me. It was so painful letting those old mindsets go, but when I did, I found a freedom I had never known. Suddenly, I was talking to God as if He were a great friend. I opened my heart and shocked myself at how intimate I allowed my conversation to be with Him. That's when I knew I was healing in how I perceived God.

You can heal from your past too. It's a process, but you must keep pursuing that intimate relationship with Him. Remember God is not a human being; we cannot use the same rules for Him as we do for people. Don't allow people to discolor the brilliance of the Lord. Study the hymns to help you see Him. Play the hymns for Him. Think about the words and allow Him to stir your heart and soul and finally, accept His love for you.

I'm reminded of a quote from Janette Oke's book (that was later made into a movie), Love Comes Softly, in which one of the characters says, "Love isn't always fireworks. Sometimes love comes softly."36 They were speaking of romantic love, but it could apply to other contexts of love, including spiritual.

You must still the chaos in music and life and surrender it all to Him. That's what music and hymns are all about.

Many of our grandparents were taught that the Bible is the foundation of truth. They knew how to be "still" before God off and on throughout the day and kept an open line of communication between them and the Creator every day. They knew people weren't God, nor themselves. They humbled themselves and let Him lead, even in difficult times.

Maybe it's not our grandparents' generation that was special, maybe it was the fruits of living a Biblical life, fully surrendered, and seeking Him to fill their emotional voids, including love. That's attainable for us today, too.

Our grandparents' generation may be slowly fading out, but the legacy of the hymns remains to help shape us and future generations. What if we had a relationship with the Lord like our grandparents did? How would our lives be changed? How would music be changed in us, toward others? What can you do to make that change happen in and through you? What a blessing to have their example for us to look to.

A Bible verse that became a personal chant for me in college is from 1 Samuel 16:7 "But the LORD said to Samuel, "Do not look at his appearance or at his physical stature, because I have refused him. For the LORD does not see as man sees; for man looks at the outward appearance, but the LORD looks at the heart."

My challenge for you as we come to the end of this book is to bring your heart to God each time you sit down to practice or perform your music. We are all broken musicians; blessedly, God loves to use broken people for His glory. He sees the person within and is ready to refine and use you to build His Kingdom; yes, even through your imperfect music!

With God, healing your brokenness is possible. I have found some tools that have helped me so much in my musical and personal journeys, but I have to work on those things day by day. It's a process; continuing to choose God every day is a choice. It may be slow, painful, or ugly in the healing process walking through each day, but not doing anything is not progress. Eventually, you must come to a point where you choose to say, "I surrender all!" That's when your life will truly begin to change.

Questions to Ponder:

• What is the biggest hurdle you must overcome in your life? Something rooted and deep? Personal or musical?

• How will you overcome it? What are steps you can take?

• Is there anything in your personal life that you need to draw closer to the Lord? How will you go about doing that?

• Is there anything in your musical life that you need to draw closer to the Lord or work through? How will you go about doing that?

• Is He still good?

How Much Blood I'd Need
(Words copyright 2022 and Music copyright 2025 by Julie Crowe)

[Verse 1] Hurting beyond attempted repair
I walked in life with enslaving snares
Surrendering my guarded heart
Was the only way to let life start.

[Chorus] Now I see how patient is He
Dying He knew how much blood I'd need
To wash the wounds of my broken heart
Of unfair thoughts that kept us apart.

[Verse 2] I tried my best to push Him away
And I could never get Him to sway
Even in moments of ugly blame
His love carried me just the same.

[Verse 3] Often I think on the very hour
People I knew deterred me sour
But holding every weakness in part
He gives me strength to live what He starts

[Verse 4] Giving up what I couldn't carry
Was the best choice even if scary
Accepting His love set me free
Nurturing His love to grow in me.

Please visit and subscribe to my new YouTube channel for music, inspiration, and more: www.youtube.com/stringsofhope-vo2pd

How to Accept Jesus as Your Lord and Savior

It's as simple as ABC: Acknowledge, Believe, Confess.

- Acknowledge you are a sinner and need a Savior.
- Believe that God sent His Son, Jesus, to die for you and the sins of the world; Jesus rose again on the third day after He hung on the cross for our sins.
- Confess to God that you need a Savior and want Him to come into your heart.

A prayer could look like this:

> Dear God, I know that I am a sinner and I have done wicked things before you, and I know I need a Savior. I believe You sent Jesus to die on the cross for my sins

and that He rose again on the third day. I accept what Jesus did for me and want Him to come into my heart and life and change me from the inside out. Please, Lord Jesus, come into my life and save me. Thank you, God, for loving and saving me. In Jesus' Name I pray, A men.

After you've prayed this prayer, start reading your Bible, attending a Bible-based church, and praying every day. God didn't promise us an easy road, but He promised He would always walk it with us. We never have to be lonely again.

The Gravitation of Private Lessons

When I first graduated college, the music lessons I taught leaned heavily to classical music with Christian influences. We would pray before we began (a habit a private violin teacher had in our lessons), and I would be more laid back but expected students to do what they had been asked to practice. We would do all the usual things after praying — scales, arpeggios, sometimes etudes, and end the lesson with a piece the student was working on. Over the years, my students shifted from mostly experienced to beginners and my method of teaching lessons changed too.

I went from expecting students to conduct rigorous studies of music on their own to being more compassionate as I watched more and more students get burned out because of perfectionism. I began slowly shifting my focus from "There is only one way to study this piece of music" to "Know your physical and emotional limitations in this season of life, strive to do your best, and play for God's glory." Lessons shifted from Classical to hymn-and-duet-heavy, Christian-based lessons inspired by my 80+ year old student, Nancy.

These lessons look like working on a hymn together, playing a duet of that hymn, fellowshipping, and creating goals to strive for, with an overall goal of worshipping God through music at home and in church. Sometimes I will also offer topical studies in music. I may touch on classical or classical-style pieces, but I mainly focus on how lessons can be an act of worship and striving for excellence, playing skillfully, and being content in the season of life the student is in.

I never really felt I belonged in the Classical Music world, it's just not who He made me to be. I'm just now beginning to glimpse some of the reasons I may think and understand the world the way I do, but He used everything, the techniques, the studies, and the music lessons to make me who I am today. The walk that God calls you into, He calls and equips along the way, and sets up people to be there, waiting for you to encourage, challenge, and help you to grow and flourish. What if there is someone waiting on you, to help you in your walk? God made us social creatures with a need of a relationship with Him first, then others.

Biblical Encouragement for the Christian Musician When You:

Compare yourself to another musician
    2 Corinthians 10:12
Get stuck in a rut
    Galatians 1:10

Are prideful

    Philippians 2:3

Are afraid of performing

    Deuteronomy 31:6

Question why you must practice

    Psalm 33: 3

Forget why you play

    Psalm 150:4

Forget Who gets the glory

    1 Corinthians 10:31

Are worried

    Philippians 4:6-7

Expect perfection from yourself

    Romans 3:23

Forgot your worth

    Psalm 139:13-18

References

Kosarkova, Alice, Klara Malinakova, Jitse P. Van Dijk, and Peter Tavel. "Childhood Trauma and Experience in Close Relationships Are Associated with the God Image: Does Religiosity Make a Difference?" International Journal of Environmental Research and Public Health 17, no. 23 (November 28, 2020). https://doi.org/10.3390/ijerph17238841. Accessed on July 7, 2023.

Barnett, Tim and Childers, Alisa, The Deconstruction of Christianity: What It Is, Why It's Destructive, and How to Respond. Audiobook. (Tyndale Elevate, 2024). Chapter 3: Rerun. Accessed on February 19, 2024.

Whittemore, Jessica. "A Study of Music: Music Psychology, Music Therapy, and Worship Music." Senior Thesis, Liberty University, 2019. Accessed on July 7, 2023.

Hymnary.org. "Come, Ye Sinners, Poor and Needy," n.d. https://hymnary.org/text/come_ye_sinners_poor_and_needy_weak_and. Accessed on July 1, 2023.

Allen, Jennie. Get Out of Your Head: Stopping the Spiral of Toxic Thoughts. WaterBrook, 2020. Accessed on June 23, 2022.

Allen, Jennie. Get Out of Your Head: Stopping the Spiral of Toxic Thoughts. WaterBrook, 2020.
Chapter Accessed on June 19, 2022.

Hymnary.org. "Turn Your Eyes upon Jesus," n.d. https://hymnary.org/text/o_soul_are_you_weary_and_troubled. Accessed on July 1, 2023.

Matthew 5:48 Commentaries: "Therefore You Are to Be Perfect, as Your Heavenly Father Is Perfect.," n.d. https://biblehub.com/commentaries/matthew/5-48.htm. Accessed on September 30, 2022.

TerKeurst, Lysa. "When I'm Desperate for God to Give Me All of the Details..."Https://Www.Facebook.Com/OfficialLysa/Photos/a.427520367693/10156895055707694/?Type=3, June 5, 2021. Accessed April 18, 2022. https://www.facebook.com/OfficialLysa/photos/a.427520367693/10156895055707694/?type=3.

Hymnary.org. "Never Alone," n.d. https://hymnary.org/text/ive_seen_the_lightning_flashing. Accessed on June 30, 2023.

Dougherty, Melissa. "What's the Oldest Lie in the Book? With Melissa Dougherty." CrossExamined.Org FB Group (Official), July 1,

2023. Accessed July 1, 2023. https://www.facebook.com/groups/1
571557166387771/.

Hymnary.org. "Just a Closer Walk With Thee," n.d. https://hym
nary.org/text/i_am_weak_but_thou_art_strong. Accessed on July 1,
2023.

"The Essence of Sin Is Man Substituting Himself for God, While
the Essence of Salvation Is God Substituting Himself for Man." Cr
ossExamined.Org FB Group (Official), June 28, 2022. Accessed June
30, 2023. https://www.facebook.com/photo/?fbid=307331163293
4649&set=a.1376576842608145.

Nancy, Interview. September of 2020.

Whittemore, Jessica. "A Study of Music: Music Psychology, Music Therapy, and Worship Music." Senior Thesis, Liberty University, 2
019.

TerKeurst, Lysa. "Trustworthy: Overcoming Our Greatest Struggles to Trust God." p. 170; 173; 176. LIfeway Press, 2019. Accessed on
Decemeber 19, 2019.

Allen, Jennie. Get Out of Your Head: Stopping the Spiral of Toxic
Thoughts. Audiobook. Waterbrook; Illustrated edition, 2020. Accessed on October 20, 2021.

Hymnary.org. "Just as I Am, Without One Plea," n.d. https://h
ymnary.org/text/just_as_i_am_without_one_plea. Accessed on June
30, 2023.

Barnett, Tim. "If You Claim to Be a Follower of Jesus, but Only Believe What Jesus Believes as Long as He Agrees with You, Then You Are Not Following Jesus, You Are Following Yourself." Red Pen Logic With Mr. B, July 3, 2023. Accessed July 3, 2023. https://www.facebook.com/redpenlogic.

Nancy, Interview. September of 2021.

Chilton, Brian, "Emotional Doubt and How to Combat It," Cross Examined, October 12, 2018, https://crossexamined.org/emotional-doubt-and-how-to-combat-it/. Accessed on January 14, 2024.

Hymnary.org. "Amazing Grace! (How Sweet the Sound)," n.d. https://hymnary.org/text/amazing_grace_how_sweet_the_sound. Accessed on July 1, 2023.

Hymnary.org. "Joyful, Joyful, We Adore Thee," n.d. https://hymnary.org/text/joyful_joyful_we_adore_thee. Accessed on July 2, 2023.

Hymnary.org. "Come, Thou Fount of Every Blessing," n.d. https://hymnary.org/text/come_thou_fount_of_every_blessing. Accessed on July 2, 2023.

Hymnary.org. "Great Is Thy Faithfulness," n.d. https://hymnary.org/text/great_is_thy_faithfulness_o_god_my_fathe. Accessed on July 3, 2023.

Hymnary.org. "My Hope Is Built on Nothing Less," n.d. https://hymnary.org/text/my_hope_is_built_on_nothing_less. Accessed on July 5, 2023.

Hymnary.org. "Are You Washed in the Blood?," n.d. https://hymnary.org/text/have_you_been_to_jesus_for_the_cleansing. Accessed on July 5, 2023.

The National Association for Christian Recovery. "Recovery from Childhood Trauma," December 15, 2017. https://www.nacr.org/abusecenter/recovery-from-childhood-trauma-2. Accessed on July 7, 2023.

Hymnary.org. "Standing on the Promises," n.d. https://hymnary.org/text/standing_on_the_promises_of_christ_my_ki. Accessed on July 5, 2023.

Hymnary.org. "Blessed Assurance," n.d. https://hymnary.org/text/blessed_assurance_jesus_is_mine. Accessed on July 6, 2023.

"God Doesn't Want Us to Stay Stuck..." Lysa TerKeurst, September 8, 2021. Accessed September 10, 2021. https://www.facebook.com/photo.php?fbid=446048010221709&set=pb.100044495407015.-2207520000.&type=3.

Barnett, Tim and Childers, Alisa, The Deconstruction of Christianity: What It Is, Why It's Destructive, and How to Respond. Audiobook. (Tyndale Elevate, 2024). Chapter 3: Rerun. Accessed on February 19, 2024.

Whittemore, Jessica. "A Study of Music: Music Psychology, Music Therapy, and Worship Music." Senior Thesis, Liberty University, 2 019.

Oke, Janette. Love Comes Softly. Hallmark Entertainment; Alpine Medien Productions; Larry Levinson Productions; Faith & Values Media, 2003. https://www.imdb.com/title/tt0345591/.

Mt. Gallagher Baptist Church, Jacob Schultz, Guest Speaker, 31:26-56:34, February 25, 2024, https://www.youtube.com/watch?v=sDXpC8SYk1Y.

www.ingramcontent.com/pod-product-compliance
Lightning Source LLC
Chambersburg PA
CBHW031423120626
46545CB00006B/2252